CHALCEDON CONTEMPORARY ISSUES
3

The Influence of Historic Christianity on Early America

by

Archie P. Jones

CHALCEDON FOUNDATION
VALLECITO, CALIFORNIA 95251

Copyright 1998

by

Archie P. Jones

Printed on acid-free paper.

All rights reserved

No part of this book may be
reproduced in any form without
permission in writing from the publisher.

ISBN # - 1-891375-02-4
The Influence of Historic Christianity onEarly America

Printed in the United States of America

Published by Chalcedon Foundation
P. O. Box 158
Vallecito, CA 95251

CONTENTS

Editor's Introduction 1
    by Andrew Sandlin

Introduction 4

The Medieval Centuries 8

The Protestant Reformation 22

Religion and Culture 28

Education 32

Science 38

Literature 41

Political Thought 45

Law, Legal Thought, and Legal Education 49

Independence 52

Religious Liberty in a Christian
Ethical Context 57

State Constitutions, Declarations of Rights and
Bill of Rights 60

The Articles of Confederation 62

The Constitution and the Bill of Rights 65

A Tradition of Christian Civil Government and Law 70

Charity and Welfare 77

Benevolence and Missions 79

A Great Heritage 82

Editor's Introduction
by Andrew Sandlin

One of the most tenacious and pernicious myths of our times is that the Founding of the United States was a dedicated exercise in secularization by Deists, rationalists, and freethinkers who wanted to subvert any form of Christian political order, breaking decisively with the inherited Christian civilization of Europe. This myth, trumpeted by everyone from politicized Supreme Court justices to sectarian or conspiratorial conservatives who dismiss or deny the plan facts of history, has become folklore in today's United States, and a useful ideology for those who wish to banish any form of Christianity from any place except between any single individual's two ears. It is a supreme instance of a historic revisionism in the humble service of an ideology.

And it is not supported by the facts.[1]

It is true that the Founders relied somewhat on classical (mainly Roman) jurisprudence, even more so than an inherited Puritan ethic, and did not fashion a specifically biblionomic (Bible-based) state; neither did Calvin and Zwingli for that matter. The fact that they did not is no justification for the charge that they were disingenuous secularists. It is because we today think only in terms of a centralized civil order that we tend to err in imputing malevolent motives to overtly Christian Founders who, for example, omitted references to Christ in the Federal Constitution as a means to ensure the free exercise of Christianity.

All of the states (as the colonies) had Christian establishments of some sort, and several had established churches. The bedrock Calvinist (and other) clergy were in the forefront of the battle to avoid explicitly religious language in the Federal Constitution *because they didn't want the Feds messing with their state establishments.* It just so happens that these early Americans had a libertarian strain we today sorely lack. The federal government was not the civil be-all-and-end-all for them as it is for too many (including Christians) today, and they resisted any attempt of the Feds and the proposed Constitution to meddle with their explicitly Christian state establishments.

It is hard for Christians suckled on *USA Today*, The Capital Gang, Dan Rather and Bill Clinton's ultra-federalism to understand this salient fact, but they do *need* to understand it.

Thomas Woods is surely correct, therefore, in concluding his review (*Modern Age*, Winter, 1997) of Kramnick and Moore's *The Godless Constitution* by noting:

> [I]t is an unstated but palpable nationalism on the part of Kramnick and Moore that renders them unable to breakout of a self-imposed either-or dichotomy: *either* the federal government permits an established church *or* even minor expressions of religious belief—including nondenominational benedictions at graduation ceremonies—are prohibited to every community in America. The possibility that the Framers may have envisioned a position between these extremes, that practices forbidden to the central [Federal] government may be perfectly licit at the state and local level, never enters their constitutional calculus. *The Godless Constitution* ultimately brings to mind Disraeli's famous description of one of his opponents: "He had only one idea, and it was wrong."

In the present work, Archie Jones exhibits the profound influence of Christianity on numerous facets of early American life—from science and literature to law and the Constitution. Indeed, the Founding and early United States cannot be understood apart from the deep influence of Christianity; for, while it was a daring experiment in constitutional democracy, it was equally an extension of the inherited tradition of Western Christian civilization. The social secularization of the last two decades in the United States, therefore, represents a distinct break with the Christian-influenced Founding, and the vanguard of today's secularists can find in the Founding no comfort of precedent in their attempt to eviscerate Christianity from American life.

Jones's work stands as a stark declaration to the imperviousness of a history resistant to reinterpretation by ideologues whose goal is nothing less than full-scale revolution. Their vested interest in revisionism is to obscure from the minds of devout American believers their glorious Christian heritage: after all, if these

Christians are convinced of a Christian Founding, they may wish to tap its roots in an effort to restore a Christian culture *today*.

It is *this* prospect that rabid secularists cannot abide.

Christians *will* overturn the regnant secular regime, and restore the Christianity that animated most of the Founders. The facts which the present work recounts will contribute to that great end.

---

[1] M. E. Bradford, "Religion and the Framers: The Biographical Evidence," *Benchmark*, Fall, 1990, IV; Joseph H. Brady, *Confusion Twice Confounded* (South Orange, 1955); David J. Brewer, *The United States: A Christian Nation* (Smyrna, GA [1905], 1996); Daniel L. Dreisbach, "The Constitution's Forgotten Religion Clause: Reflections on the Article VI Religious Test Ban," *Journal of Church and State*, Vol. 38 [Spring 1996], 261-295; *idem.*, "In Search of a Christian Commonwealth: An Examination of Selected Nineteenth-Century Commentaries on References to God and the Christian Religion in the United States Constitution," *Baylor Law Review*, Vol. 48, No. 4 [Fall, 1996], 927-1000; *idem.*, *Religion and Politics in the Early Republic*, ed., (Lexington, 1996); John Eidsmoe, *Christianity and the Constitution: The Faith of Our Founding Fathers* (Grand Rapids, 1987); Stanton Evans, *The Theme is Freedom: Religion, Politics, and the American Tradition* (Washington, D. C., 1994); Charles S. Hyman and Donald S. Lutz, eds., *American Political Writing During the Founding Era* (Indianapolis, 1983, 2 volumes); Archie Jones, "The Myth of Political Polytheism [A review of Gary North's *Political Polytheism*]," *Journal of Christian Reconstruction*, Vol. 14, No. 1 [Fall, 1996], 271-286; R. J. Rushdoony's *This Independent Republic* (Fairfax, VA [1964], 1978); *idem.*, *The Nature of the American System* (Fairfax, VA [1965], 1978); Herbert W. Titus, *The Constitution of the United States: A Christian Document* (Chesapeake, 1997).

Introduction

© 1998 Archie P. Jones
Copyright includes data files on diskettes.

Early American society did not spring from nothing, nor did it simply shape itself once the various peoples who settled what became these United States came to these shores. Early American society was largely a product of English society, with lesser influences, varying with localities, from the societies of the people who explored, colonized and settled the English colonies, intermarried, to some extent, with the Indians, and, to a far greater extent, with each other, and made new homes, livelihoods and communities for themselves and their posterity in this part of the "New World": Scottish, Irish, French, German, Dutch, Spanish, Swedish, and other peoples of Western Europe. The peoples of Europe brought certain views of God, of life and the world, and of men and things, to their new homes in America. However, they and their descendants continued to be influenced by religious and philosophical ideas and culture from their former homelands and from Europe in general. Thus, throughout most of our history American intellectual thought has followed European intellectual ideas.[1]

Culture is the common view of the world, of life, and of the nature of God, men, and things, and the values, beliefs, and customs derived from that common view shared by a people. Culture is therefore a product of the religion or religious philosophy of a people. It is the Biblical principle that "as a man thinketh in his heart, so is he" worked out on a collective level. Early American culture was thus largely a product of European culture, modified by the predominant influence of English culture. As a part of European culture, early America's roots were deeply imbedded in certain limited aspects of the pagan cultures of ancient Greece and Rome; in the Hebrew culture of the Old Testament; and, to a much greater extent, in the Christian culture of the tumultuous, yet productive, medieval period and the Protestant Reformation.[2]

It would be amazing if Christianity had not had a decisive influence on Western civilization and American civilization. The

Lord Jesus Christ is certainly the most influential man who has ever lived. Christianity's teaching that man was created in the image of God—a great truth reaffirmed in the Incarnation in the fact that Jesus is fully human and fully God—denied the ancient and modern non-Christian denigration of the importance of human life and raised the value of human life in the eyes of men. The Bible's teaching about woman exalted the female and protected her against abortion, rape, and many other kinds of abuse. Biblical faith produced a balanced view of sex—its purpose being for procreation and for the mutual enjoyment of husband and wife—placed sex within the realm of the family, protected the members of the family against sexual abuse, and established high moral standards for sexual conduct. Christian faith and moral teachings not only changed countless individuals' lives radically for the better, but also civilized (as it continues to do) numerous barbaric, cruel, immoral nations and peoples. The example and teachings of Jesus and the word of God's teachings about Christian ethical duties motivated men to attitudes and works of compassion and mercy. Biblical faith led directly to the idea of popular education and resulted in the development of the university and modern science. The example of Jesus and belief in the teachings of the Bible created a strong work ethic, protected private property and the accumulation of capital, and laid the moral foundation for free enterprise economics. Christian faith also gave the world political freedom, liberty under the rule of law, and representative government. Jesus' concern for the wellbeing of people, His healing miracles, and the Bible's ethical teachings rescued men from the disease-yielding fruits of sin, gave people a health-producing way of life, and, with Christianity's founding of modern science, laid the foundation of modern medicine and hospitals. In addition, Christianity led to the creation of written languages, formed or transformed the literatures of the peoples of the West, and produced great works of literature, music, and art.[3] Christianity did all of this—and more—gradually over the centuries since the advent of Christ, despite much adversity.

By God's grace and providence, triumphing over the pagan religions of the ancient world and the repeated persecutions of pagan Roman emperors, Christianity grew, became dominant in the Roman Empire, then expanded outside that declining Empire. Western civilization is the new and far greater civilization which, ultimately as a result of the work of the Holy Spirit and secondarily as a consequence of the labors of the church, grew out of the civilization of the fallen western half of the Roman Empire. As a part of Western civilization, early America's culture was also a product of aspects of the cultures of the pagan tribes that inhabited or invaded, then settled Europe, and were Christianized during the declining years of the Empire and the long medieval centuries;[4] of the partly pagan, partly Christian Renaissance; of the Protestant Reformation; of the Roman Catholic Counter-Reformation; and of subsequent religious and political developments in Europe and in England.[5] The medieval period and the Protestant Reformation were clearly the two most fundamental and formative of these cultural influences.

---

[1] This point is common to intellectual and cultural histories of America, and to histories of American intellectuals' ideas, though scholars differ on the amount of time lag between European intellectual fashions and fads and those of American intellectuals.

[2] Russell Kirk, *The Roots of American Order* (LaSalle, Illinois: Open Court, 1974).

[3] D. James Kennedy and Jerry Newcombe, *What If Jesus Had Never Been Born?: The Positive Impact of Christianity in History* (Nashville: Thomas Nelson Publishers, 1994) and *What If the Bible Had Never Been Written?* (Nashville: Thomas Nelson Publishers, 1998). On Christianity's affirmation of the value of human life and its repeated struggles against ancient and modern non-Christian denigration of the value of human life and against the horrible practice of abortion, see George Grant, *Third Time Around: A History of the Pro-Life Movement from the First Century to the Present* (Brentwood, Tennessee: Wolgemuth & Hyatt, 1991).

[4] History is a continuous flow of events which does not strictly lend itself to the artificial divisions which historians and other commentators on history have created. As Ronald A. Wells, has noted in *History Through the Eyes of Faith: Western Civilization and the Kingdom of God* (Washington, D.C.: Christian College Coalition, 1989), 47-58, the notion that the "medieval period" or the "middle ages" is a distinct epoch between either the man-centered ancient period or the time of

the early church and the "modern era or age" does not fit the historical evidence. There was actually a continuity in the development of the church and the Christianization of the peoples of Europe from the last centuries of the Roman Empire through what we know as "the medieval period."

[5] See Christopher Dawson, *The Making of Europe: An Introduction to the History of European Unity* (Cleveland and New York: Meridian Books, [1958] 1961), *Religion and the Rise of Western Culture* (Garden City, New York: Image Books/Doubleday, [1950] 1958), *The Formation of Christendom* (New York: Sheed & Ward, 1967): Roland H. Bainton, *Christendom: A Short History of Christianity and Its Impact on Western Civilization*, vol. 1, *From the Birth of Christ to the Reformation* (New York: Harper Colophon Books, [1964] 1966): Kenneth Scott Latourette, *Anno Domini: Jesus, History, and God* (New York and London: Harper and Brothers, 1940); Eugen Rosenstock-Huessy, *Out of Revolution: Autobiography of Western Man* (Norwich, Vermont: Argot Books, 1969); and Kirk, *The Roots of American Order*.

The Medieval Centuries

During the medieval period (from approximately A.D. 500 to A.D. 1500)[1] the Holy Spirit and the church built upon the previous work of Christians in the Roman Empire and extended Christianity far beyond the boundaries of the Empire. During its early centuries and the early medieval period, the work of the church in formulating, teaching, and defending the basic creeds of Christianity was crucially important. Men's basic assumptions about God, Christ, salvation, the fundamental nature of things, and ethics have important consequences, and Biblical truth has vitally important consequences not only for salvation of individual souls but also for social and political order.[2] Preserving the work of the early church, Christians of the medieval period laid the foundation of Christian faith and culture in Europe and in England, gave Europeans the idea of a Christian society, and made the societies of Europe part of a larger Christian civilization, Christendom.

Having become predominantly Christian, the old Roman Empire split into two Christian civilizations that shared common religious and ethical assumptions, yet quarreled over theological and political issues.[3] Western civilization grew out of the western half of the Roman Empire, particularly after the decline and fall of that realm. The eastern half of the old Roman Empire continued to call itself the Roman Empire, but is known to us as the Byzantine Empire. It exerted some important influence on the West, but theological differences, mutual sins, and historical events worked to separate it from the West.

The civilization of the West was dominated by the Latin church, which later became the Roman Catholic Church, but was characterized by a theoretical and practical division of functions between ecclesiastical government (the church) and civil government (the state). There were some power struggles between the two, though both acknowledged they were under the authority of God and His law-word. After Charlemagne's failure to establish a Christian empire in the West, civil government was much more fragmented than in the East. The feudalism upon which later national monarchies were established was a complex system of mutual responsibilities exercised by civil governments which were essentially local. The West saw many more struggles between competing civil government rulers than did the East, as well as more power struggles between church and state. Western civilization encompassed the diverse peoples of Western, Central, Northern and Southern Europe.

The Byzantine Empire, which was at first predominantly Greek but later composed of many peoples, had a dynamic history and lasted almost a thousand years longer than the western Roman Empire. It preserved and extended civilization during the centuries when civilization was at a low ebb in the West, and it led the eastern half of Europe out of paganism and savagery. For ten centuries this great Christian empire protected the West and Christianity from onslaughts arising from the steppes and the East: Slavs, Bulgars, Huns, Avars, Persians, and Moslem Arabs and Turks. Byzantine civilization was based on both the Bible and Greek philosophy, was dominated by the emperor, who ruled the church, and was religiously dominated by what became the Orthodox Church. Byzantine civilization and culture influenced Russia, Eastern Europe—Serbs, Croatians, Bulgars, Moravians, Khazars, Narentians, Hungarians—and Christians in the Near East. In the centuries before and after its final destruction in 1453, Byzantine civilization influenced Western civilization directly and indirectly through its codification and Christianization of Roman law (forbidding the exposure of infants, encouraging chastity, protecting women, marriage, children and the family, requiring equal punishment for rich and poor, and making life easier for slaves) and the work of its fleeing scholars, who brought ancient (and other) Greek texts to the West, thus preparing the way for the Renaissance.[4]

Throughout the medieval period the church and its monasteries were the greatest forces working to Christianize and civilize the pagan peoples of Western and Eastern Europe.[5] Christian faith, morals, and views of the world and of life were spread by missionaries, monks, priests, merchants, and others. Having been evangelized, the Celts of Ireland established monasteries that became centers of learning, and sent missionaries to the Anglo-Saxons. Having been converted, the Irish and English sent missionaries to the Germanic peoples of the continent. The

Norsemen (Swedes, Danes, and Normans) were gradually converted by the Christian peoples they settled among and by missionaries sent to Scandinavia. In Eastern Europe, Slavs, Russians, Magyars, and Bulgars were evangelized and discipled. Christianity even spread to the east of Mesopotamia—as far as India and China—though it was wiped out in some areas as a result of Mohammedan conquest.

During these eventful centuries, Christians imparted a clearly (though not perfectly) Biblical view of the world and of life to the peoples of Europe, which influenced religion, philosophy, ethics, customs, political thought, politics, law, civil government, literature, art, music, architecture, science, technology, and other aspects of Western culture. The Bible was more widely available to medieval men and Biblical knowledge was more widely diffused than we have been led to suppose by popular writers.[6] Christianity both spread and increased in its influence on the cultures of the peoples of the West. The church made theology the queen of the sciences and reoriented philosophy toward a search for goals and standards of ethics different from those of the ancient Greek and Roman pagans. It taught Christian ethics condemning pride, lust, fornication, envy, avarice, sloth, deceit, perjury, theft, murder, and other sins common to all men and commonly approved by the pagan tribes. Where the church triumphed, human sacrifice and slavery disappeared. It tried to enforce its teachings by precept and example. Even where it tried to synthesize Aristotle's philosophy and the Bible, as in Thomas Aquinas' system, it imposed Christian ethics on pagan ethical standards and sought to retain a Christian theology and philosophy.[7]

The church preserved classical learning during and after the Empire's decline and fostered a series of renaissances based on a combination of Christian culture and classical learning which gave rise to European culture.[8] Notable among these was the renaissance in the twelfth century, long before the famous Renaissance of the sixteenth century.[9] Churches and monasteries became centers of education and culture, and the church gave civilization not only schools but also the university and specialized schools of medicine and law. Building on the work of Augustine, Christian rhetoricians Christianized the purposes and content of rhetoric, putting it to work in the defense of the Faith, the edification of the faithful, and the advancement of Christian truth.[10]

The struggle between Christian and pagan purposes of rhetoric illustrates the fact that Christian preservation of the works of the ancient pagans cut both ways. It preserved great works of the mind, which stimulated men to think about many areas of life, and could be used for Christian purposes. However, it also preserved anti-Biblical presuppositions and premises, which could misdirect the thinking of Christians and be used by non-Christian thinkers to undermine and overthrow Christian thinking, culture, ethics, and institutions. The struggle between Christian thought and man-centered, anti-Biblical thought is fundamental to the mindset of man in Western civilization. It was evident in the Renaissance, particularly in the Italian Renaissance, and is perhaps most clearly seen in the works of Machiavelli, the great Renaissance political philosopher and dramatist who masked his opposition to God and Christian ethics under a claim of neutral, objective observation.[11] It would be developed more fully in eighteenth century Enlightenment rationalism and in nineteenth and twentieth century Western man-centered thought, which is in rebellion against God[12] and His law-word, and is intellectually and morally relativistic, collectivistic, and implicitly totalitarian since it denies all ethical standards by which limits can be placed on the power of the rulers of civil government.[13]

The modern rebellion against God and His law—a continuation of the ancient theological and ethical rebellion launched by Adam and continued by the ungodly line of Cain through all times—is especially clear in legal and political thought and practice. It is an attempt to overthrow our medieval and Reformation Christian legacy of ethical, legal, and political thought.

During the medieval period, Christian influence changed the ethical, legal and political thinking of the peoples of the West, together with that of most of their intellectual leaders and rulers. The church not only developed a system of canon law, derived basically from the Bible, for itself, but also made a great effort to influence the content of all areas of medieval law. Christianity became basic to Western law.[14] In England, Christian belief and ethics became the basis of the common law through multitudes of judicial decisions from the twelfth century on.

Because Christianity taught that God rules history providentially and that Jesus Christ, the second person of the Trinity, is the King of Kings and Lord of Lords, Christians came to understand that God is in authority over all civil governments and their rulers, that rulers must obey His law, and that the authority and power of rulers must be limited in accordance with God's law. Because Christianity taught that Jesus Christ is the only Savior, Christians knew that neither a ruler nor a civil government could be the savior of men, and concluded that the power of civil governments and their rulers must be limited. Hence Christianity worked to de-divinize the state, and to deny to the civil government and its rulers any claim to be divine, to be as gods, or to exercise arbitrary or unlimited power. These conclusions were reinforced by Christianity's teaching that all men are radically and adversely affected by original sin: that all men are sinners, rebelling against God's laws, and seeking to be their own gods. This, too, implied that the power of civil governments and their rulers must be limited in accordance with God's standards of ethics and law.[15]

The Biblical fact of the revelation of God's law in His creation, in "nature," indicated that men can know God's standards of justice, of good and evil. This conclusion, combined with elements of Greek and Roman ethical thinking, led to the creation of theories of "natural law" and to the Christianization of the content of the laws revealed in "nature." The fact that God has revealed His holy law more clearly, propositionally, and extensively in Scripture meant that He has made His law available for all—citizens as well as those in positions of authority—to know and obey. These concepts led to the central principle of medieval legal and political philosophy: that the king is under God and His law and may make no laws that violate God's laws. Christian thinking also developed and taught the ideas that civil governments are formed upon the basis of a covenant under God between the people and their rulers; that the rulers of civil government derive their powers, under God, from the consent of the governed; that rulers must keep their covenants with the people they rule; that the people are not bound to obey the unjust, ungodly laws of covenant-breaking rulers; and that the people may resist and overthrow covenant-breaking rulers who seek to be tyrants. During the medieval period, the West, especially England, developed institutions which functioned to check and balance the power of monarchs and so also to preserve freedom. The church became the most influential social institution having spiritual authority over every person, including kings, as well as the authority to resist and rebuke civil government rulers for their sins. The nobility claimed its rights based on a complex network of feudal covenants[16] and on Christian principles underlying these covenants. Possession of weapons and wealth by nobles, cities, and towns made it necessary for kings to get the consent of their subjects in order to impose taxes, thus limiting taxation. Institutions of representative government grew from Christian ideas and from the practical outworkings of the above ideas. Independent courts like the common law courts of England were another source of resistance against unjust, arbitrary rule by kings. Moreover, nobles and citizens, aided by the church, acted upon the basis of such convictions to resist unjust, arbitrary rule by kings, and to maintain the supremacy of law by forming written documents like the Magna Carta, a key document of modern constitutional government.[17] Medieval legal thought, working with Roman law and medieval feudal realities (lord and vassal relationships of authority and subjection based on covenants), then with the fourteenth century struggles between Italian cities and the emperor, and finally with the work of the great Spanish legal theorists of Salamanca, developed modern constitutional legal theory and made the right to resist tyranny universal by arguing that the power of the state, under God, has its origin in the people, that kings are bound by the law, and that states or nations are under the authority of fixed legal principles.[18] All of these ideas meant that the power of civil government must be limited. Their practical outworking meant that the medieval heritage is one of liberty under law—God's law—and of rightful resistance against injustice and revolution against tyranny. Liberty was central to medieval political thought in the West.[19]

In addition to restricting civil government, the church sought to restrict warfare, to exempt non-combatants from the destruction of war, and to bring about peaceful reconciliation of conflicts. The attempt to modify the conduct of the warriors of the warlike peoples of the West by the application of Christian principles was a fundamental to the development of the code of chivalry.[20]

The influence of the church was both theoretical and practical. Monasteries became centers of work as well as education. Monks labored to clear land, drain swamps, and encourage agriculture and animal husbandry as well as to pray, study, and meditate. The church encouraged work, advocated stability of money, and made men conscious that they were accountable to God for how they acquired and used their property. Christian teachings about God, man, creation and God's providence made it possible for men to use the rudiments of ancient scientific writings and laid the foundation for modern, self-sustaining science.[21] The teaching that God created all things from nothing and rules them by His divine providence made men see creation as being rational and orderly. The idea that God is a God of order underscored the order and lawfulness of the creation. The fact that God created man in His image and the teaching that man is to have dominion over the earth and all its creatures made men see that they are able to understand God's handiwork in His creation. It also induced them to labor to discover part of the glory of God in the workings of His creation, and led them to work to learn how to use the processes of God's world for man's advantage, to God's glory. The teaching that man is to do good works, among other things to alleviate the suffering of his fellow men, also stimulated scientific investigation and the application of scientific discoveries to human purposes. For these reasons—despite modern anti-Christian propaganda to the contrary—modern self-sustaining science originated only in Western civilization, during the medieval period. During the medieval period multitudes of men, acting upon the basis of such Christian beliefs, studied various aspects of the creation, leaving voluminous written records of their work.[22]

As a consequence of such views, many important developments in agriculture, technology, and commerce occurred in the Christian West during the medieval period.[23] The seventh century, the time of Charlemagne, saw the development of a balanced system of animal and cereal crops, the widespread use of the heavy plow in northern Europe, and an attitude that man could have mastery over nature.[24] By the end of the ninth century the nailed horseshoe had been introduced, providing important protection for horses' hooves and enabling them to work more efficiently. The addition of the collar-harness during the next several centuries enabled faster and more efficient horses to replace oxen in working fields and pulling loads. Great improvements in wagons followed the invention of the modern harness and resulted in improved transportation capacity and speed. Invention of the new three-field system of crop rotation in the seventh century joined with the invention of the heavy plow and the replacement of the ox by the draught-horse to make Northern European agriculture vastly more productive than either the Teutonic or the Latin agricultural systems. Besides the use of legumes in the three-field crop rotation system, the proteins produced in the legumes perfectly supplemented the proteins present in the common grains, resulting in a new, better type of food supply. These developments were basic to Northern Europe's great increase of population, the growth and increase of its cities, and the rise in industrial production and commerce, and helped to shift the focus from Southern to Northern Europe.[25]

During the early medieval period men's attitude toward the creation changed from a relatively passive acceptance of "nature" to a view which endorsed the exploration of "natural" phenomena so that the forces in the creation could be used for human purposes. The greater liberty of men in the medieval West enabled them to innovate, to try and develop new techniques and technologies.[26] In the later medieval period, men in the West developed far more diverse sources of power than had been available to any previous culture. This produced a revolution in machine design which put these sources of power to many uses and formed a concept of power technology—the use of machines to tap the sources of energy in creation for human use. They developed the power of moving water, wind, expanding gases, weights, and springs far more fully than had been done before, and experimented and developed machines to control the use of this power. In the eleventh and twelfth centuries they applied the cam to many functions: mills were used for fulling, tanning, laundering, sawing, crushing; for operating bellows for blast furnaces, triphammers, grindstones; for reducing pigments for paint, pulp for paper, and mash for beer. In the thirteenth century they added the spring and treadle as sources of power. In the fourteenth century they developed complex systems of gears and applied them to a variety of uses. In the fifteenth century they developed the crank, the connecting-rod, and the governor to make the conversion of reciprocating motion into continuous rotary motion. By exploring these sources of power and designs of machinery, they developed such diverse things as improved waterwheels, tidal mills, windmills, cannons, guns, trebuchets, weight-driven clocks, rotary grindstones, crossbows, flywheels, treadle-operated looms and lathes, pipe-organs, spring-operated saws and lathes, spinning wheels, mechanical clocks, the double-compound crank and connecting rod, the carpenter's bit-and-brace, and the windlass.[27] Eyeglasses, an important innovation of the medieval period, enabled men to read longer and be more productive.

These technological advances contributed to the great commercial revolution that occurred in the West between the tenth and fourteenth centuries. Between about 950 and 1350, vastly improved agriculture led to increased population and released income for business investment. The growth of an enterprising merchant class—particularly in Venice, Genoa, Milan, and Florence—supplied men who were deeply interested in trading ventures. Improved transportation—more flexible, complex road networks, the horse-collar, horseshoes, axled pairs of wheels, new kinds of vessels for many purposes, improved methods of ship construction, increased sizes and numbers of ships, the keel, and improved navigational instruments—made commerce more efficient. Growing seapower made markets more accessible to Western merchants. Increased use of credit and the development of new kinds of commercial contracts made capital more available for commercial ventures. Double-entry bookkeeping made business calculations far more accurate. The development of insurance provided a more rational allocation of investment capital. By the eleventh century, the West had surpassed both Byzantium and the Islamic Empire in wealth; and the center of economic power had shifted to the Western Europe. This was the first time in history an underdeveloped society had developed itself mostly by its own labors.[28]

Accompanying these technological advances was an increasingly broader outlook on the world, as men of the late medieval period sought markets beyond the Mediterranean and began exploring the west coast of Africa. The major impetus to explore was a desire to bypass the Arab monopoly of trade routes to obtain the spices, gold, precious gems, and silk of India, China, and the islands of the Far East to reap the profits from these precious commodities. Evangelization of the heathen and prevention of the expansion of Mohammedanism were also major motivations of European exploration, conquest, and colonization.

Not all of these technological and economic advances were made by Christians, of course, nor were all motivated by Biblical concerns. Yet as a whole they can be seen as outworkings of Christian faith, the fruits of Biblical thinking applied to various areas of life and work, and even as the blessings of God on a people who, by-and-large, had faith in Him and sought to obey His commandments.

God led His church to do all these things though the West, the church, and Christianity were repeatedly threatened by a series of disasters throughout the medieval period. From the fifth through the tenth centuries, and even into the sixteenth century, the western and eastern halves of Christendom were beset by a series of disastrous invasions by barbaric pagan peoples. In the fourth and fifth centuries the western half of the declining Roman Empire was troubled by invasions of various Germanic tribes. In the fifth century Attila and the Huns wreaked havoc in Europe, as did the Alani on a lesser scale. In the sixth century the Lombards and the Avars took their destructive turn, followed by the invading Slavs and Bulgars. Also, in that century, the Arabs, motivated by the new religion of Islam, invaded the West and occupied Spain. During the eighth, ninth, and tenth centuries, much of the West was plagued by the raids and invasions of the Scandinavian pagans, the Norsemen or Vikings. In the eleventh and twelfth centuries the Seljuk Turks created an empire in the East which threatened both the Byzantine Empire and Western Europe. From the thirteenth to the fifteenth centuries the Mongols ravaged Eastern Europe and parts of the Byzantine Empire and threatened the West. From the thirteenth through the sixteenth centuries the Ottoman Turks threatened both the eastern and western halves of the lands dominated by Christianity. These barbarian invasions were, of course, judgments of God used for His purposes, some of which were directly constructive. Wars fought within Christendom added to the devastation. Periodic plagues—other judgments of God—brought death and destruction to the peoples of Christendom. All of these were caused by and compounded by the destructive nature of the sins of the individuals, rulers, and peoples of the areas dominated by Christianity.

Despite these difficulties, God worked through the church and the lives of Christians to make Western civilization clearly (though not perfectly) Christian in its religion, ethics, law, political thought, literature, art, music, science, and culture in general. These developments laid the foundation for both Roman Catholicism and Protestantism. Though God did not choose to perfect the Christianity of any of the peoples of Europe, He used the work of the church during the medieval centuries to transform the cultures of the peoples of Europe from pagan to Christian cultures and to advance Christianity and Christian civilization. Through the influence of the church He laid the theological, cultural, economic, and technological foundations of the modern West.

---

[1] As noted above, the division between the "medieval" (middle) period and the years which preceded it is artificial. It should also be noted that the definition of the end of the medieval period is arbitrary. Historians who like to give credit to the revival of ancient Greek learning and other developments of the centuries before 1500 to the Renaissance of the sixteenth century tend to date the end of the medieval period a century or two earlier than 1500. Walter Kirchner placed its origin "sometime between 375 and 732" and said that during the fourteenth, fifteenth and sixteenth centuries the "Middle Ages" merged, "almost imperceptibly" into modern times. *Western Civilization Since 1500*, Second Ed. (New York: Barnes & Noble, 1975), 11.

[2] See Rousas John Rushdoony, *The Foundations of Social Order: Studies in the Creeds and Councils of the Early Church* (Presbyterian & Reformed Publishing Co., 1972). See also his *The One and the Many: Studies in the Philosophy of Order and Ultimacy* (Craig Press, 1971).

[3] Dawson, *The Formation of Christendom*, 252-256, argues that the fundamental difference which caused the great schism between the Eastern and Western churches was the West's opposition to the

caesaropapism of Justinian and subsequent Byzantine emperors: the exaltation of the authority of the ruler of civil government over that of the Church. He classifies issues such as the primacy of the Roman see and the celibacy of the clergy as "only matters of law and ritual order." Yet differences in these matters derived from differing interpretations of Scripture and disputes similar to the iconoclastic controversy in the Byzantine Empire which manifested theological differences between that empire and the Latin West.

[4] On Byzantine history and culture, see J.M. Hussey, *The Byzantine World* (New York: Harper & Row, 1961), Steven Runciman, *Byzantine Civilization* (New York: Meridian Books, [1933] 1960), Rene Guerdan, *Byzantium: Its Triumphs and Tragedy* (New York: G.P. Putnam's Sons, 1957), A.A. Vasilev, *History of the Byzantine Empire 324-1453* (Madison: University of Wisconsin Press, 1952), David Jacobs, *Constantinople: City on the Golden Horn* (New York: American Heritage Publishing Co./ Harper & Row, 1969), and Harold Lamb, *Theodora and the Emperor: The Drama of Justinian* (Garden City, New York: Doubleday, 1952).

[5] Bainton, 117, 118.

[6] S.R. Maitland, *The Dark Ages: Essays Illustrating the State of Religion and Literature in the Ninth, Tenth, Eleventh, and Twelfth Centuries* 2 vols. (Port Washington, New York: Kennikat Press, [1889] 1969), passim.

[7] Kirchner, 13.

[8] Philippe Wolff, *The Cultural Awakening* (New York: Pantheon Books, 1968).

[9] Charles Homer Haskins, *The Renaissance of the Twelfth Century* (Cleveland and New York: The World Publishing Co., [1957] 1966).

[10] James A. Herrick, *The History and Theory of Rhetoric: An Introduction* (Scottsdale, Arizona: Gorsuch Scarisbrick Publishers, 1997), 126-144.

[11] As Leo Paul DeAlvarez has pointed out, Machiavelli's longest work, *Discourses on the First Ten Books of Titus Livius*, or *Discourses*, his most famous and influential work, *The Prince*, and his play, *La Mandragola*, all, by clear implication, deny God and the validity of His law as the ethical standard for the individual, society, and civil government. They call for the use of the form of the church to overthrow Christianity and advocate the freedom of the ruler of civil government to use force and deceit judiciously to do whatever he desires to do. The best study of Machiavelli's thought as fundamental to modern man-centered political philosophy is Leo Strauss, *Thoughts on Machiavelli* (Seattle: University of Washington Press, [1958] 1969).

[12] See Albert Camus, *The Rebel: An Essay on Man in Revolt* (New York: Vintage Books, 1958).

[13] The best work on this is John H. Hallowell, *Main Currents in Modern*

Political Thought (New York: Holt, Rinehart and Winston, [1950] 1953).

[14] Harold J. Berman, *Law and Revolution: The Formation of the Western Legal Tradition* (Cambridge, Massachusetts: Harvard University Press, 1983).

[15] For a fuller discussion of the implications of Christian faith for law and politics, see Rousas John Rushdoony, *Christianity and the State* (Vallecito, California: Ross House Books, 1986). See also his *Law and Liberty* (Vallecito: Ross House Books, 1980), *The One and the Many*, *The Institutes of Biblical Law* (Presbyterian and Reformed Publishing Co./ The Craig Press, 1973), and *Law and Society: Volume II of The Institutes of Biblical Law* (Vallecito, California: Ross House Books, 1982).

[16] For a lucid explanation of the importance of this phenomenon and its relationship to American history, see Rousas John Rushdoony, *This Independent Republic: Studies in the Nature and Meaning of American History* (Nutley, New Jersey: The Craig Press, 1964), 9-22.

[17] See M. Stanton Evans, *The Theme Is Freedom: Religion, Politics, and the American Tradition* (Washington, D.C.: Regnery Publishing, Inc., 1994).

[18] Reuben C. Alvarado, "Fountainhead of Liberalism," *Contra Mundum*, no. 10 (Winter, 1994), 23-24.

[19] R.W. and A.J. Carlyle, *A History of Medieval Political Theory in the West* 6 vols. (London: 1936).

[20] Latourette, *Anno Domini*, 54-94.

[21] On the Biblical basis of modern science, see Henry M. Morris, *The Biblical Basis of Modern Science* (Grand Rapids: Baker Book House, 1984); and D. James Kennedy and Jerry Newcombe, *What If the Bible Had Never Been Written?* (Nashville: Thomas Nelson Publishers, 1998), 101-110.

[22] On the medieval foundation of modern self-sustaining science, see Rev. Stanley L. Jaki, "Science and Censorship: Helene Duhem and the Publication of the 'System du monde,'" *The Intercollegiate Review*, vol. 21, no. 2 (Winter, 1985-86), 41-49, in which he notes that Pierre Duhem compiled 120 500-page notebooks taken from medieval scientific manuscripts; *The Origin of Science and the Science of Its Origin* (New York: John Wiley and Sons, 1977); *Science and Creation: From Eternal Cycles to an Oscillating Universe* (Princeton, N.J.: Stanley L. Jaki); and *The Road of Science and the Ways to God* (Chicago: University of Chicago Press, 1976). On the philosophical problems of man-centered science, see Rousas John Rushdoony, *The Mythology of Science* (Nutley, New Jersey: The Craig Press, 1964); Gordon H. Clark, *The Philosophy of Science and Belief in God* (Nutley New Jersey: The Craig Press, 1964); and Vern S. Poythress, *Philosophy, Science and the Sovereignty of God* (Phillipsburg, New Jersey: Presbyterian and Reformed Publishing Co., 1976).

[23] See, for example, Lynn White, Jr., *Medieval Technology and Social Change* (London: Oxford University Press, [1962] 1971) and Robert S. Lopez, *The Commercial Revolution of the Middle Ages 950-1350* (Englewood Cliffs, New Jersey: Prentice-Hall, 1971).
[24] White, 56-57.
[25] White, 57-78.
[26] Otto Scott, untitled lecture on history at the Biblical Horizons Conference, Trinity Presbyterian Church, Valparaiso, Florida, July 29, 1998.
[27] White, 79-134.
[28] Lopez details these developments.

The Protestant Reformation

In making Christianity the religion of Western civilization, making the Bible available to so many people in the West,[1] devoting so much energy to teaching Christian ethics, and countenancing so many movements for reform of the church, the church had set forth standards by which it and its officials could be judged. When the church departed from fundamental Christian standards of faith and morals, movements to reform the church arose within the church. When, during the late medieval period, the church developed a body of doctrine which departed from the teaching of the Bible about the locus of authority and the means of salvation and tolerated many practices which clearly violated the Bible's and the church's teachings on morality, it created a situation which was ripe for the development of movements to reform the church. Those movements culminated in the Protestant Reformation.

The Protestant Reformation was not a movement against the medieval period as a whole. It was not an attempt to do away with all that had been accomplished for Christ; nor did it seek to destroy the improvements in man's earthly condition that Christianity had produced during the medieval period. The Protestant Reformation was a great movement within the church against unbiblical doctrines and immoral practices that had developed in the church during the medieval period. Positively, it sought a consistently Biblical faith and practice. It worked to replace the late medieval standard of Scripture and an oral tradition supposedly passed down from Peter and the apostles to the rulers of the church with a return to the Bible as the only infallible standard of faith and practice. Although the Reformation gave rise to diverse bodies of thought, the mainstream did not reject the idea that the church is to disciple the nations for Christ, or the idea that it is a fundamental duty of the church to produce a Christian society. Nor did the Reformation reject the triumphs of historic Christianity which were contained in the beliefs, institutions, customs, laws, and ways of life of Western civilization. It sought to build on the accomplishments of Christendom, to call the church back to the Scriptures as the rule of faith and life, and to apply the Scriptures to all areas of life.

Lutheranism was the earliest manifestation of the Protestant Reformation. However, Calvinism, the system of theology taught by or derived from John Calvin, spread faster, was more international, and was far more influential in Europe and America. Originating in Geneva, Calvinism spread to Switzerland, Spain, Poland, Hungary, Italy, France, the Netherlands, Germany, Hungary, England, and Scotland before it spread to America and elsewhere.[2] Although usually thought of as a theology concerned with the famous "Five Points" of salvation by the sovereign will and grace of God,[3] Calvinism is actually a theology which attempts to apply Biblical principles to all areas of thought and life. Consequently, its impact was not merely "religious" in the narrow sense, but cultural. It impacted not merely the church, but also evangelism and missions, the family, education and learning in general, science, political thought, social thought, law, economic life, politics, rhetoric, and culture as a whole because it sought to transform all areas of culture to Biblical standards for the glory of God. Thus it built on the accomplishments of the medieval period and sought to reform not only theology and the church but also all areas of life that were not conformed to the teachings of the Scriptures.[4]

Calvinism was a great force for evangelism. The great forerunners of the Reformation were, in principle, Calvinists, for they taught essentially the same doctrines. The great national reformers—Zwingli of Switzerland, Calvin of France, Cranmer of England, Knox of Scotland, and Luther of Germany—were Calvinistic in their key doctrines.[5] Calvinism spread very rapidly throughout Western Europe. The great revivals in the modern history of Europe and these United States were either predominantly or largely Calvinistic.[6] Though Calvinism was not the expressed theology of all the peoples who established colonies in this hemisphere, evangelization and Christianization of non-Christian peoples in general, and of the Indians in particular, was a basic and prominent motive in the exploration, conquest, and settlement of the "New World."

Calvinism was certainly a great force for morality. It was marked by its concern for conscience and its concomitant sense of duty. Calvinistic teaching and preaching appealed to settled convictions based on scriptural duty, not on fleeting emotions. Consequently, Calvinists were known for high standards of conduct, moral rectitude, and moral courage. They produced many people of high moral character and many glorious martyrs for the Faith, many who stood for Christ and Biblical truth in the face of religious persecution by church and king.[7]

Calvinism was also a great influence on the rise of modern science. Like Lutheranism and Protestantism in general, it continued and reinforced the medieval Christian doctrines of creationism, God's divine providence, the orderliness of the creation ("nature") and the ability of man to understand "nature." Calvinists joined with Roman Catholics and other Protestants whose Biblical view of the world involved a rejection of the authority of Aristotle, which entailed a rejection of his view of the structure of nature, thus freeing men from the Greek deification of nature and giving them a different outlook about nature. This "gave a religious sanction to the development of technology, that is, to the dominion of nature by human art," which benefited science and technology greatly in the sixteenth and seventeenth centuries.[8] With Francis Bacon, Christianity in general and Calvinism in particular encouraged men to engage in scientific research, combining science and technology, as a religious duty of charity: to overcome ignorance, restore man's dominion over nature, and use knowledge to serve the good of man by alleviating the hardships of human life.[9] In addition, Calvinists joined other Christians in rejecting the Greek denigration of the manual trades, endorsed manual trades as godly callings, taught tradesmen and common people science, urged common people to gather scientific data, and worked with tradesmen to develop scientific instruments and conduct scientific experiments.[10] Protestants, especially Calvinists, "Puritans" in a general sense, or members of Reformed churches, endorsed science as a loving religious duty—to glorify God, to make godly use of their talents, to serve God ethically out of gratitude for salvation, and to see the work of God in His creation. These Calvinists were far more numerous among scientists than the number of Protestants or Calvinists in the total population would indicate.[11]

Calvinism was also a great political force, a force for justice and liberty.[12] Its theologians and thinkers produced the lion's share of the great Protestant political essays that revived the medieval doctrines of the right and duty to resist tyranny.[13] The Puritans, English and American Calvinists, developed and defended the idea of liberty of conscience.[14] Calvinists stood and fought against severe tyrannical persecution in France, the Netherlands, Scotland, and England. In England Calvinists, opposing Arminian-directed religious persecution and perfidious, tyrannical behavior by Charles I, gave posterity what Otto Scott has rightly termed the Great Christian Revolution, which overthrew the tyrant, set up a republican government, established liberty, and was a key precedent for the American Revolution and our Constitution.[15]

The importance of Calvinism to early American civilization and culture cannot be rightly doubted. Not only Christian but also non-Christian, not only Protestant but also Roman Catholic historians have affirmed this.[16] The Pilgrims and Puritans who founded our most celebrated and perhaps most influential colonies and helped to settle Maryland and other colonies were Calvinists, as were the Presbyterians, Huguenots, and Baptists who settled throughout the colonies, and the Reformed groups who settled in the middle colonies. The Anglicans, who founded Virginia and the Carolinas and were influential in the South, in New York and elsewhere, had a Calvinistic confession of faith in their Thirty-nine Articles (though not all Anglicans were Calvinists). Even the tiny minority of Roman Catholics were culturally Calvinistic and intellectually medieval, being much influenced by the surrounding Protestant culture.[17] Loraine Boettner estimated that about two-thirds of early Americans at the time of our American Revolution were "trained in the school of Calvin."[18] Ahlstrom, in the standard work on our religious history, said that the American colonies had become "the most thoroughly Reformed, and Puritan commonwealths in the world," declared that "Puritanism provided the moral and religious background of fully 75 percent of the people who declared their independence in 1776," and noted that if one were to include all the people "whose forebearers bore the 'stamp of Geneva' in some broader sense, 85 or 90 percent would not be an extravagant estimate."[19]

---

[1] As Maitland has noted in *The Dark Ages*, passim, the Bible was in fact far more available to the people of the West during the so-called "Dark Ages" than we have been led to suppose.

[2] See W. Stanford Reid, ed., *John Calvin: His Influence on the Western World* (Grand Rapids: Zondervan, 1982), and John T. McNeill, *The History and Character of Calvinism* (New York: Oxford University Press, 1954).

[3] Among the many works on the sovereignty of God and the "Five Points" of Calvinism are Arthur W. Pink, *The Sovereignty of God* (Grand Rapids: Baker Book House, [1930] 1973); Gordon H. Clark, *Biblical Predestination* (Phillipsburg, New Jersey: Presbyterian and Reformed Publishing Co., 1969); Patrick Hues Mell, *A Southern Baptist Looks at Predestination* (Grace Baptist Fellowship, n.d.); Loraine Boettner, *The Reformed Doctrine of Predestination* (Philadelphia: Presbyterian and Reformed Publishing Co., [1932] 1972); John L. Girardeau, *Calvinism and Evangelical Arminianism: Compared as to Election, Reprobation, Justification, and Related Doctrines* (Harrisonburg, Virginia: Sprinkle Publications, [1890] 1984). On Arminianism see also Otto Scott, *et.al.*, *The Great Christian Revolution: The Myths of Paganism and Arminianism* (Vallecito, California: Ross House Books, 1991).

[4] In addition to Reid and McNeill, see Abraham Kuyper, *Lectures on Calvinism* (Grand Rapids: William B. Eerdmans, [1898] 1958) and N.S. McFetridge, *Calvinism in History* (Edmonton: Still Waters Revival Books, [1882] 1989).

[5] McFetridge, 101.

[6] McFetridge, 103-112.

[7] McFetridge, 73-92.

[8] R. Hooykaas, *Religion and the Rise of Modern Science* (Grand Rapids: William B. Eerdmans, [1972] 1974), 67, 68.

[9] Hooykaas, 67-74.

[10] Hooykaas, 75-97.

[11] Hooykaas, 98-149.

[12] McFetridge, 1-72. See also Douglas F. Kelly, *The Emergence of Liberty in the Modern World: The Influence of Calvin on Five Governments from the 16th Through the 18th Centuries* (Phillipsburg, NJ: Presbyterian & Reformed Publishing Co., 1992).

[13] Quentin Skinner, *The Foundations of Modern Political Thought: Volume Two: The Age of Reformation* (Cambridge: Cambridge University Press, 1978), notes that the first statement reviving medieval doctrines of the right of resistance against injustice and tyranny was produced in 1530 by the Lutherans of Magdeburg, Germany; then the Calvinists continued the political tradition of resistance against tyranny. See also Julian W. Franklin, trans. and ed., *Constitutionalism and Resistance in the Sixteenth Century: Three Treatises by Hotman, Beza and Mornay* (New York: Pegasus, 1968); Junius Brutus, *A Defense of Liberty Against Tyrants;*

or, Of the lawful power of the Prince over the People and of the People over the Prince: Vindiciae Contra Tyrannos (Edmonton, Alberta, Canada: Still Waters Revival Books, [1579] 1989); Samuel Rutherford, *Lex, Rex: or The Law and the Prince* (Harrisonburg, Virginia: Sprinkle Publications, [1644] 1982); and Richard L. Greaves, *Theology and Revolution in the Scottish Reformation: Studies in the Thought of John Knox* (Grand Rapids: Christian University Press, 1980).

[14] L. John Van Til, *Liberty of Conscience: The History of a Puritan Idea* (The Craig Press, 1972).

[15] *The Great Christian Revolution: How Christianity Transformed the World* (Windsor, New York: The Reformer, [1994] 1995). On Arminian theology's political opposition to Calvinism and to freedom, see Reuben C. Alvarado, "Fountainhead of Liberalism," 15-25, a review-essay refuting Charles S. McCoy and J. Wayne Baker, *Fountainhead of Federalism: Heinrich Bullinger and the Covenantal Tradition* (Louisville, Kentucky: Westminster/John Knox Press, 1991).

[16] See Boettner, *The Reformed Doctrine of Predestination*, 382-399.

[17] Erik von Kuehnelt-Leddihn, "The Western Dilemma: Calvin or Rousseau?," *Modern Age* XV (Winter, 1971), 49.

[18] Boettner, 382-383.

[19] Sydney E. Ahlstrom, *A Religious History of the American People* (Garden City, New York: Doubleday and Co., 1975), vol. 1, 169.

Religion and Culture

From the founding of the colonies through the years of the "Civil War" and beyond, Christianity was virtually the only religion professed by Americans.[1] To be sure, there were unbelievers, like the shiftless inhabitants of "Lubberland" discussed by William Byrd of Westover or like later celebrated rationalistic thinkers. Yet these were never the majority of the American population and, more importantly, they never set the tone of early American society, culture, or thought. The religious profession of the vast majority of early Americans was Christian and Protestant. At the time of our War for Independence there were only about 20,000 Roman Catholics out of a population of perhaps three million Americans, and there were far fewer Jews than there were Roman Catholics. Although the Unitarian Controversy rocked New England Congregationalism in 1801, the Unitarians (who called themselves Christians) did not organize as a separate entity until 1825. Though the percentage of Roman Catholics increased dramatically in the 1840s, America remained a clearly Protestant nation until at least 1890 though by this time modernism and some heretical sects diluted the Protestantism.

Contrary to what we have often been told or led to believe by some Christian as well as by many non-Christian scholars, early America was a Christian society.[2] Christianity was not only predominant among the people, it was also widely influential on early American society and thought. From 1607 until at least 1776 Christianity was as important as economics and politics in shaping American life and values (and Christian belief shaped both economic and political activity). Though there was some decline before and after the Great Awakening of the mid-1700s, the vitality of Christianity was strong in the southern and middle colonies, as well as in New England throughout the colonial years. In the eighteenth century churches extended their influence through all parts of the colonies, including the frontier. A majority of adults attended church regularly; social, political, and cultural as well as "religious" values were associated with churchgoing.[3] Though there was some decline in Christian influence as a result of the War for

Independence, the series of revivals during the Second Great Awakening in the early 1800s renewed the strength of Protestant Christianity and, as Perry Miller said, "rolled through the years before the Civil War like a juggernaut," influencing even American judges' and lawyers' understanding of the law.[4]

Though ancient Greek and Roman thought were important influences on early American culture, legal, and political thought, neither was so fundamental nor so influential as was Christianity.[5] Early American culture and thought had deep roots in the medieval period and were not merely Protestant but largely Calvinistic. Calvinism, of course, is a continuation of the thinking of the early church and particularly of Augustinianism. Puritanism is the best known and was the most influential form of early American Calvinism. It has been seen as the most important influence on American national character,[6] though it could be argued that Presbyterianism was a more important influence on early American national character.[7] Yet not only Congregationalists but also Presbyterians, members of Reformed churches, many Anglicans—all of whose denominations stressed education—and Baptists were Calvinistic in their thinking. Since as many as ninety percent of Americans in 1776 had Calvinistic backgrounds, and since Calvinism was concerned not only with applying the Bible's teachings to salvation but also to all areas of thought and life, it is easy to see why early American culture and thought was dominated by Calvinistic ideas.

---

[1] By "religion" is meant a view of the world and of life based on a set of presupposed ideas taken on faith. This incorporates and describes all systems of thought, whether they be called religions or philosophies, for philosophical systems, too, are based on presupposed ideas about the fundamental nature of reality, about God, men, and things. While it is fashionable in some Christian circles to distinguish Christianity from all other religions by saying that Christianity is the truth and all other religions are false, and while such a statement is true, the statement obscures the fact that all systems of human thought are based upon presuppositions which are not proven but rather are accepted by faith.

[2] See Gary DeMar, *America's Christian History: The Untold Story* (Atlanta: American Vision Publishers, Inc., 1993). As DeMar, 3-10, notes, to

say that America was Christian is not to say that it was perfect, and those Christian historians who attempt to deny that America was a Christian society by defining a Christian society as one which is perfectly Biblical or Christian create an impossible—and unBiblical—definition in terms of which their churches could not be termed Christian.

[3] Patricia U. Bonomi, *Under the Cope of Heaven: Religion, Society and Politics in Early America* (New York: Oxford University Press, 1986), 87-92 and passim.

[4] Perry Miller, *The Life of the Mind in America: From the Revolution to the Civil War* (New York: Harcourt, Brace & World, 1965), especially 3-98, 164-202.

[5] Richard M. Gummere, *The American Mind and the Classical Tradition* (Cambridge: Harvard University Press, 1963) overemphasizes the influence of the classical tradition on our culture and thought. More accurate assessments of the relative influence of Christianity and classical culture in American thought and politics are found in Kirk, *The Roots of American Order*, 11-50, 137-300, 332-246, 415-440; Ellis Sandoz, *A Government of Laws: Political Theory, Religion, and the American Founding* (Baton Rouge and London: Louisiana State University Press, 1990); Thomas Cuming Hall, *The Religious Background of American Culture* (Boston: Little, Brown and Co., 1930); William Warren Sweet, *Religion in the Development of American Culture* (New York: Charles Scribner's Sons, 1952); E.C. Wines, *The Hebrew Republic* (Marlborough, New Hampshire: Plymouth Rock Foundation, [1980], 1998); B.F. Morris, *Christian Life and Character of the Civil Institutions of the United States* (Philadelphia: George W. Childs, 1864); Ahlstrom, *A Religious History of the American People*; C. Gregg Singer, *A Theological Interpretation of American History* (Presbyterian and Reformed Publishing Co., [1964] 1982); Rousas J. Rushdoony, *This Independent Republic: Studies in the Nature and Meaning of American History* (Nutley, New Jersey: The Craig Press, 1964); Tim J. Campbell, *Central Themes of American Life* (Grand Rapids: William B. Eerdmans Publishing Co., 1959); A. Mervyn Davies, *Foundation of American Freedom* (Nashville: Abingdon Press, 1955); John W. Whitehead, *The Stealing of America* (Westchester, Illinois: Crossway Books, 1983); Ernest Lee Tuveson, *Redeemer Nation: The Idea of America's Millennial Role* (Chicago: University of Chicago Press, 1968); Cushing Strout, *The New Heavens and New Earth; Political Religion in America* (New York: Harper and Row, 1974); Ralph Barton Perry, *Puritanism and Democracy* (New York: Vanguard Press, 1944); Clinton Rossiter, *Seedtime of the Republic: The Origin of the American Tradition of Political Liberty* (New York: Harcourt, Brace and Co., 1953); and Nathan O. Hatch, *The Sacred Cause of Liberty:*

Republican Thought and the Millennium in Revolutionary New England (New Haven: Yale University Press, 1977).
[6] Joseph Gaer and Ben Sigel, *The Puritan Heritage: America's Roots in the Bible* (New York: Mentor Books, 1964); Sacvan Bercovich, *The Puritan Origins of the American Self* (New Haven: Yale University Press, 1975).
[7] C. Gregg Singer, "The Scotch-Irish in America," in Reid, 269.

Education

From its earliest days until well after the founding of the deceptively labeled "free public education" in Massachusetts in the late 1830s, early American education was dominated by Christianity. The Puritans' concern that all be educated and that those who are ablest be more highly educated is well known. Civil government encouraged (but did not control) education in colonial New England. The Puritan concern for godly education was united with an appreciation of the value of the written word. This resulted in Boston becoming an early leader in publication.

Colonial education was overwhelmingly dominated by Christian views and values. The Puritan concern for education was shared by Presbyterians and other Christians, Calvinistic and otherwise, outside of New England. The Bible, "the single most important cultural influence in the lives of Anglo-Americans" throughout the seventeenth century, was believed to be "universally relevant,"[1] and though there were classical (ancient Greek and Roman) elements to colonial education,[2] Bible-based teaching was predominant throughout the colonies. There was not a great change in the basic pattern of American education for many years after independence,[3] though establishment of "free public education," the rebellion of many intellectuals against the Bible, and the gradual de-Christianization of the textbooks would eventually change the content of American education.

Education in early America was accomplished in several ways. Education began at home, and many families homeschooled their children (by the parents, a relative, or a tutor) for all or part of the children's education. In the home children and family servants were taught reading, the catechism, and the local civil laws. Apprenticeship indentures were another means of education since the agreements obliged masters to provide for the moral and spiritual welfare of the apprentices they took into their homes as well as the occupational instruction of the indentured.

Particularly in New England, the town provided a schoolmaster for elementary education. Later towns provided a grammar school to prepare boys for college. In the grammar school, the Bible was carefully studied in its original languages, and the works of ancient writers (mainly in Latin) were read.[4] In the middle of the eighteenth century the academy was developed from the grammar school. The academy added new subjects of practical value but kept the Christian emphasis of the grammar school. The "public" high school appeared in the late 1830s and gradually replaced the academy outside the South. It gradually became de-Christianized or "secular" in its emphasis, but not until long after it had been established.[5]

The church was a fundamental method of education, for the sermon was the chief means of popular education. Sermons (particularly in the churches which required a more learned clergy) were much longer and had much more content than do typical sermons today. Ministers were among the most respected people in society, and their ministries often included public lectures or sermons. Ministers often tutored students or established denominational or non-denominational Christian schools. In addition, there were schools, operated for profit, which taught Christian views and values. In the South there were "field schools" operated in buildings erected on fields donated for the purpose of education and using teachers supported by local parents. In the middle colonies education was accomplished mainly through parochial schools because these colonies had been settled by diverse denominational groups.[6]

Until about 1750, the Bible, especially the New Testament, and the Psalter were the basis of practically all reading matter in schools. The famous *New England Primer*, which was said to have "taught millions to read and not one to sin," was in virtually every home and in all bookstores. It was the basic elementary text for all the colonies that were not under the control of the Church of England.[7]

After the framing and ratification of the Constitution, American education remained largely private until the middle decades of the nineteenth century, when "free public education" began to make its way in New England and spread across the states of the North. The motivation of the leaders of the crusade for free public education was Unitarian, anti-Christian, socialistic, and utopian.[8] However, these leaders did not publicize their motives and proceeded gradually to accomplish their goals. Still, early

American education remained predominantly Christian, though it had less denominational emphasis. Moreover, in every state in which it was successful, the "public education" movement was constructed "upon previous efforts of a denominational character."[9]

The American system of what the nineteenth century called "common schools" was largely an effort to harmonize the conflicting Christian denominational traditions that had previously been central to American education.[10] Mid-nineteenth century "common schools" were basically Protestant schools, with local variations, based upon the ethnic composition of the local community.[11] Because Protestants were preponderant, they found it easier to accept or support state-controlled, nonsectarian schools. Roman Catholics and members of smaller Protestant denominations found the American tradition and principle of local control to be useful for sectarian purposes when they could settle in a compact group and dominate a local community.[12]

Whether or not there were sectarian teachings in the schools, the textbooks continued to convey respect for Christianity and "prayers and scriptural readings were almost universal."[13] Although new, more secularist readers and spellers replaced the psalters, testaments, and Bibles that had dominated colonial education, the most popular new texts after 1800 also sought to convey Christian principles. Noah Webster's best-selling *American Dictionary of the English Language* (1828) sought to give Biblical definitions to words, and his *Elementary Speller*, which sold a million copies annually, was outspokenly Christian in character.[14] The famous *McGuffey's Readers*, first published in 1836, provided texts for millions of American schoolchildren and shaped the minds of four-fifths of school children for seventy-five years. The first edition (1836-1850) provided a view of the school curriculum for the first half of the nineteenth century, before the "public school" movement took hold in the North. These readers were strongly theistic and Calvinistic; they stressed salvation, righteousness, and piety. Their content emphasized first religion, then morality, and then knowledge. They were God-centered, saw God as the Lord of both the Old and the New Testaments, and assumed that all true knowledge of God comes from the Bible. They stressed that God is uniquely revealed in Jesus Christ, that He is the key to meaning and purpose in men's lives, that God morally governs His creation, and that His providence is the key to understanding both the "natural" world and the affairs of men and societies.[15] The process of de-Christianization of the *McGuffey Readers*, reducing God to a Unitarian concept, began with the second edition (1857) and was completed with the third edition (1879).[16]

Though Unitarian educational theorists worked behind the scenes to de-Christianize textbooks and schools, a somewhat diluted Protestantism continued to survive in school texts and educational periodicals. Many practices such as state-required Bible reading and prayers in the public elementary and secondary schools, and the teaching of Christianity in state colleges and universities, prisons, reformatories, asylums, orphanages, and homes for soldiers continued.[17] Christianity remained predominant, for, as Curti has said:

> [A]s in the colonial period, there was a fairly general conviction that a chief aim of schooling is to provide the necessary basis of instruction in religion. No great educational leader before the Civil War would have denied that intellectual education was subordinate to religious values. None would tolerate any non-Christian beliefs in the schools.[18]

Like elementary and secondary education, early American higher education was markedly Christian and Protestant. Christianity dominated college education: in the aim of education, the teaching of the Bible and theology, the conduct of daily worship services, and in the goal of forming Christian character.[19] Until at least the early nineteenth century, college education in America was distinctly Christian, Protestant, and traditional. Its form was like that of medieval higher education, being patterned after the higher education that had been typical in Christendom for nearly seven centuries, though it was plainly Protestant. It was heavily ethical, teaching Christian ethics; moreover, it applied ethics to all areas of life, including politics and law.[20]

Neither the church nor the state shied away from teaching the application of God's truth to civil government, law, or political issues. The public political sermon was a particularly important means of disseminating theological, ethical, legal, political, and historical teachings to audiences throughout the colonies and states. Ministers were highly educated men: many had two degrees; were soundly educated in Latin, Greek, and (often) Hebrew; and were liberally educated in history, the classics, literature, and science. These sermons, which continued from the early days of the colonies beyond the time of the framing and ratification of the Constitution and the Bill of Rights and were preached throughout the colonies and states, conveyed a complex, sophisticated body of theological and philosophical thought grounded in Biblical faith and Calvinism; they explored first principles and applied this basic view to the issues of the day.[21]

Early American education is a key indication that the notion that the predominance of man-centered rationalism began in pre-Revolutionary America is a myth.[22] Though its Christianity was gradually diluted, education in early America remained chiefly Christian and Protestant, doing its part to lay the foundation of a Christian, Protestant society and system of civil governments and laws by shaping Christian ethical character in the young and by teaching students to see religion, morality, civil government, science, and other areas of thought and life as being under the rule and authority of God.

---

[1] Lawrence A. Cremin, *American Education: The Colonial Experience 1607-1783* (New York: Harper and Row, 1970), 38-40.

[2] Cremin, 551; see also Gummere.

[3] On early American education and its relevance to issues of "church and state" and the First Amendment, see Archie P. Jones, "Christianity in the Constitution: The Intended Meaning of the Religion Clauses of the First Amendment," Ph.D. Dissertation, University of Dallas, 1991, 79-144.

[4] C.B. Eavey, *History of Christian Education* (Chicago: Moody Bible Institute, 1964), 196.

[5] Jones, "Christianity in the Constitution," 94; Eavey, 197.

[6] Eavey, 198-199.

[7] Eavey, 89,196.

[8] The best work on the motives behind and rise of government-controlled, socialistic education, euphemistically called "free public education," is Samuel L. Blumenfeld, *Is Public Education Necessary?* (Boise, Idaho: The Paradigm Co., [1981] 1985).

[9] Timothy L. Smith, "Parochial Education in American Culture," in Paul Nash, ed., *History and Education: The Educational Uses of the Past* (New York: Random House, 1970), 201.

[10] Smith, 201.

[11] Smith, in Nash, 201; see also Tyack, in Nash, 212, 217-219.

[12] Smith, in Nash, 196, 197.

[13] Merle Curti, *The Social Ideas of American Educators: with New Chapter on the Last Twenty-five Years* (Totowa, New Jersey: Littlefield, Adams & Co., [1935] 1966), 16.

[14] Curti, 17.

[15] John W. Westerhoff III, *McGuffey and His Readers: Piety, Morality, and Education in Nineteenth Century America* (Milford, Michigan: Mott Media, [1978] 1982), 18, 19, 76-104.

[16] Westerhoff, 19, 104-107.

[17] Curti, 18; John W. Whitehead, *The New Tyranny: The Ominous Threat of State Authority over the Church* (Fort Lauderdale: Coral Ridge Ministries, 1982), 29.

[18] Curti, 20.

[19] Eavey, 201.

[20] Edmund Walsh, S.J., *The Education of the Founding Fathers of the Republic* (New York: Fordham University Press, 1935).

[21] Ellis Sandoz, "Preface," *Political Sermons of the American Founding Era, 1730-1805* (Indianapolis: Liberty Press, 1991), xiii-xxiv. Prof. Sandoz's work on these political sermons, with his work on early American political thought, corrects much that Christians and others have been taught in church as well as in school, and should be read by all thoughtful Christians and, for that matter, by all thoughtful Americans.

[22] Jones, "Christianity in the Constitution," 105-125.

Science

As was the case in many other areas, early American interest in science was built upon the foundation laid down in the medieval period and the Reformation.[1] This interest is best seen in the Puritans, but is also evident in the work of Presbyterians, Anglicans, and members of other denominations.

Puritanism, in the broad sense including all kinds of Calvinism, was closely related to science in sixteenth and seventeenth century England. Puritanism had many adherents among the merchants, artisans, and navigators, who were highly interested in science and technology. Puritans, who wanted to Christianize all areas of life, found Francis Bacon's Biblically-based writings on science and technology very attractive. Optimistic eschatological expectations of Puritans and others saw science as a means of advancing Christ's kingdom. Many men believed that religious and scientific enlightenment must accompany each other, that religion must permeate and illuminate science. Puritanism created a climate favorable to the growth and freedom of science. The Puritans were the main source of support for the new science before the Restoration.[2] Seven of the ten scientists who were the nucleus of what became the Royal Society in England were strong Puritans. Sixty-two percent of the members of the Royal Society in 1663 were of Puritan origin, though Puritans were a minority of the English population.[3]

Scientific activity was common among learned early Americans, especially Puritans, including ministers. Puritan ministers like Cotton Mather and Jonathan Edwards, as well as other ministers and laymen, engaged in scientific studies. Ezra Stiles, president of Yale, for example, took an interest in science and corresponded with scientists. Francis Allison, a Presbyterian minister who was vice-provost of the College of Philadelphia, urged that natural history be studied in American colleges. Almost all colonial American colleges were Christian institutions, and their presidents (who were ministers) and teachers championed both comprehensive education and the teaching of the sciences. Men like Provost William Smith of the College of Philadelphia argued that the interests of Christianity would be advanced by promoting a knowledge of science. Many of the best scientists were drawn from the clergy, especially those associated with the colleges. Early Americans benefited from the greater stress which the English dissenting academies and Scottish universities placed on science; Harvard and other American colleges in the eighteenth century were influenced by them. The Reverend John Witherspoon, as president of Princeton, brought with him a high view of science.[4] Science was not neglected in early American colleges. Graduating seniors in early American colleges were examined publicly, being required to defend scientific as well as philosophical and ethical propositions.

Of course, not all ministers had basic scientific knowledge,[5] and non-Christians could and did make use of science. Still, historic Christianity transmitted an interest in science to early America, and that interest stimulated Christians and non-Christians to further scientific knowledge and its application to the betterment of the life of man.

An interesting example of this is Matthew Fontaine Maury, the Pathfinder of the Sea, who founded oceanography. Maury was motivated by his Bible-based background and view of the world to undertake his foundational studies of the sea. His favorite Psalm included the words: "O, Lord, our Lord, how excellent is Thy name in all the earth. What is man that Thou art mindful of him. . .? Thou madest him to have dominion over the works of Thy hands. . . . The fowl of the air and the fish of the seas and whatsoever passeth through the paths of the sea."[6] Maury induced naval and civilian captains to report their ships' logs' records of wind and current directions and locations. He compiled these into charts which gave a knowledge of wind direction and currents that enabled great reductions in sailing times, greatly improving navigation and commerce. He is the father of the U.S. Naval Academy at Annapolis. He studied the salinity of the ocean. His writings on the ocean taught men to see God's hand in the sky, and in the surface and the depths of the sea.[7]

Early American science education and its applications had a very practical thrust—an emphasis consistent with Christianity's teaching that the Christian is to apply Biblical teachings to the practical matters and issues of life—which can also be seen in early American literature.

---

[1] Kennedy and Newcombe, *What If the Bible Had Never Been Written?*, 100-118; Kennedy and Newcombe, *What If Jesus Had Never Been Born?*, and Morris, *The Biblical Basis of Modern Science*.

[2] Hooykaas, 135-160.

[3] Hooykas, 98-99.

[4] Brooke Hindle, *The Pursuit of Science in Revolutionary America 1735-1789* (Chapel Hill: University of North Carolina Press, 1956), 80-101.

[5] Hindle, 94-97, recounts a couple of instances of such ignorance. Muriel L. Guberlet, *Explorers of the Sea: Famous Oceanographic Expeditions* (New York: The Ronald Press Co., 1964), 12, 25, 30.

[6] Psalm 8 KJV.

[7] Guberlet, 12-31.

Literature

American literature cannot be well understood without a comprehension of the views of the world and of life that undergirded and motivated American writers and their readers.[1]

Although American literature owes much to the Renaissance, it owes its primary values to the medieval period, to the idea that the chief values of life are derived from Christian theology.[2] Like the rest of American culture, however, our literature owes even more to the Protestant Reformation, for, as the authors of the *Literary History of the United States* note, there is ample proof that "the spirit of American letters is predominantly Protestant,"[3] for the American colonies were products of Northern European Protestantism, not of the man-centered humanism of the Italian Renaissance, so early Americans' culture was a Biblical culture.[4] As Randall Stewart noted in *American Literature and Christian Doctrine*, "the Bible has been the greatest single influence on our literature," and our writers, almost without exception—orthodox or unorthodox—"have been steeped in Biblical imagery, phrasing, rhythms."[5] Calvinism, as typified by Puritanism, was the basis of our literature; it was and has been "one of the most pervasive of all influences in American life"[6] and letters.[7] It "was not an anachronism in the eighteenth century";[8] indeed, it remained influential long after Puritanism proper had declined. It affirmed the sovereignty of God over His creation; the divinity of Christ; the depth and pervasiveness of original sin in man; the divine inspiration and spiritual authority of the Bible; salvation by the grace of God alone; the sovereignty of God in predestining who will be saved and in ruling His creation and creatures by His divine providence; the responsibility of man in the fulfillment of his duties of conscientious morality, of righteous living and of doing good works to glorify God; and the legitimacy of dissent from non-Biblical rulers in church and state.[9] The influence of Puritanism was not limited to non-separatist Congregationalism, for the Calvinistic theology of the Puritans was shared by Christians of other denominations and was expressed by writers who were not strictly Puritans.

The Bible is the deepest of books, providing continual meat for the thoughtful person. Calvinism, the most fully Biblical theology, was and is an intellectually demanding, systematic distillation of God's revealed word. Calvinism attracted many of the greatest minds of the sixteenth and seventeenth centuries, and Calvinistic churches (Puritan, Presbyterian, and Reformed) demanded that their pastors be learned men and encouraged laymen to be so. Consequently, early Americans produced "the most erudite colonial literature the world has ever seen."[10] This literature was theological, inward looking, and very concerned with morality. It honored women, stressing the domestic rather than the sexual role of woman and insisting on the purity of womanhood as an ethical ideal.[11]

What the majority of the people are buying and reading does not necessarily get included in literature textbooks, for the professors who compose the textbooks choose what to include and what to exclude upon the basis of their own predilections. A telling illustration of the continuing importance of Calvinism or of generally Puritan thinking in American literature is the immense, long-lasting influence of John Bunyan's great allegory of the Christian life, *The Pilgrim's Progress*. This story of the soul's difficult, hazardous journey through life to salvation taught important ethical lessons, teaching Americans about Satan's wiles and the temptations of the world along with its theological lessons.[12] Though Bunyan was not an American, purchases of *The Pilgrim's Progress* by Americans indicate their tastes in literature.

Another important but neglected indication of the influence of Biblical Christianity and of Calvinism upon early American society and culture is Puritan minister Michael Wigglesworth's *The Day of Doom*, a didactic epic poem of 224 eight-line stanzas depicting the final return of Christ and the last judgment. Intended as a vehicle for the teaching of doctrine, this great work dramatized Christ's sudden return; the division of men between the goats and the sheep; the legal and theological arguments of the various categories of goats against their damnation, followed by Christ the Judge's theological, legal, and logical refutations of their arguments and His affirmation of the justice of God's sovereign, saving grace; the sending of the goats to eternal punishment; and the transformation of the views of the elect so that they see all of Christ's judgments as just.[13] Until the publication of Benjamin Franklin's *The Way to Wealth* (1758), *The Day of Doom* outsold all other American literary works. People looked to it as a guide to theology. Preachers quoted it in their sermons. Wise men enjoyed it. Parents read it to children. Pious people memorized it, and to know it was a sign of piety. Only the Bible and the *New England Primer* were more influential than *The Day of Doom* in colonial America.[14] The influence of *The Day of Doom* indicates clearly that Biblical Christianity, Calvinism, was still powerful in pre-"revolutionary" America and helps to explain the continuing influence of public political sermons before and after the War for Independence.

As the influence of rationalism (faith in man's unaided reason's infallibility) and romanticism (faith in the natural goodness of man) and their offshoots of Unitarianism and Transcendentalism grew, some Christians used their literary talents to counter the false, optimistic views of God, human nature, and things disseminated by non-Biblical thinkers. Nathaniel Hawthorne, who is best known for criticizing the Puritans' method of dealing with adultery and the Salem witchcraft trials, reaffirmed the Calvinistic, Puritan, and Biblical view of the deep, pervasive nature of original sin, via his short story romances like "Young Goodman Brown," "The Minister's Black Veil," "The Bosom Serpent," and "Ethan Brand." He criticized scientism (the notion that man-centered science can solve all human problems) in "The Birth-Mark" and "Rappaccini's Daughter." Having seen an experiment in communal socialist living as a participant in Brook Farm, he pilloried socialism in *The Blithedale Romance*. In "The Celestial Railroad," Hawthorne used the form and content of the continually popular Christian classic allegory *Pilgrim's Progress* to satirize notions that salvation and the Christian life are easy; that Transcendentalism and other forms of modern man-centered philosophy are anything other than falsehoods, snares, and delusions; and that Satan is not still actively deceiving people into departing from Christian faith. Thus, Hawthorne (among other things) fought against the false popular notions of his day and, like earlier Christian authors, reaffirmed basic truths of Christian doctrine.

---

[1] Rod W. Horton and Herbert W. Edwards, *Backgrounds of American Literary Thought* 2nd ed. (New York: Appleton-Century-Crofts,[1952] 1967) is helpful to such an understanding (though it is not written from a Biblical perspective), although general works on Western or European and American religious, philosophical, or intellectual and cultural history provide a sufficient foundation for understanding our literary thought.

[2] Robert E. Spiller, et.al., *Literary History of the United States: History* 3rd ed. (New York: The Macmillan Co., 1966), 9.

[3] Spiller, 12. The *Literary History of the United States* is the standard work in its field.

[4] Spiller, 12-13.

[5] Randall Stewart, *American Literature and Christian Doctrine* (Baton Rouge: Louisiana State University Press, 1958), 3.

[6] Stewart, 4.

[7] Stewart, 17.

[8] Stewart, 11.

[9] Stewart, 3-15.

[10] Spiller, 13.

[11] Spiller, 14-15.

[12] Kirk, 280, 281.

[13] When this great old work is included in today's Christian school textbooks it is presented only in a badly truncated form. For example, Jan Anderson and Laurel Hicks, *Beginnings of American Literature: Classics for Christians*, vol. 3 (Pensacola: A Beka Book Publications, 1982), 244-245, includes only seventeen stanzas of the poem, neglects to tell the reader of the work's importance and influence, and (typically, for A Beka works on American History and Literature) omits mention of the poem's Calvinistic theology.

[14] George McMichael, ed., *Anthology of American Literature*, vol., *Colonial Through Romantic*, Fifth Edition (New York: Macmillan, 1993), 135-136.

Political Thought

The basic truths of Christian doctrine were also fundamental to early American political thought. Early American political thought, of course, grew out of a long Christian tradition of political thought which is easily traceable back through the Reformation to the medieval period and, ultimately, to the Bible. The political thinking of the Puritans, certainly, is obviously traceable to the Bible, for they sought to build their political and legal thought from the Scriptures.

One indication of the Christian roots of early American political thought is a study of the sources cited as authoritative by American political thinkers who produced 916 books, monographs, pamphlets, and newspaper articles between 1760 and 1805. By far the most frequently cited source was the Bible at 34 percent. "Enlightenment" (eighteenth century) thinkers were cited as authoritative 22 percent of the time, but most of these were conservative, often Christian, legal and political thinkers, not Deists or philosophers. English Whig thinkers were cited 18 percent of the time. The common law, a basically Christian body of English law, was cited 11 percent of the time. Of the individual thinkers cited, Baron Charles Montesquieu, the French Roman Catholic political philosopher who praised English political institutions for their design to protect liberty, was cited the most often (8.3 percent). Sir William Blackstone, the conservative Anglican legal scholar was the second most cited (7.9 percent); and John Locke, the Arminian Christian political philosopher, was the next most cited (2.9 percent).[1] John Eidsmoe's survey of the thought of the most cited writers indicates that the principles that they taught "are either derived from, or at least compatible with, Christianity and the Bible."[2]

Another indication of the Christian roots and nature of early American political thinking is its content. Politics and religion have been inextricably intertwined in the American experience. Early American political thought is founded upon an awareness of the generally Christian nature of the American people and assumes the truth of the Christian view of God, the nature and capabilities of men, and politics. It has both Christian and classical (ancient Greek and Roman) dimensions, but the classical have often been mediated through early modern political writers and have been interpreted in such a way as to make them conform to Christian teachings. It had a traditionally Western and Protestant view of the individual and of the American national community. It saw the national community as having a covenantal relationship with God, and thus bound in a religious and moral relationship of obligation to Him; as having to struggle against evil, to repent for sins, to adhere to the Christian Faith and walk righteously before the Lord; and as being chastised for sins and blessed for obedience, through the workings of His divine providence. Its view of power, spirit, and virtue were Christian, as were its views of liberty and law. Early American statesmen and political thinkers sought to apply the thought of ancient and modern philosophers, the science of civil government, and the experience of history and of practical politics to the framing of our constitutions and laws in such a way that our political institutions and fundamental laws would conform to the truths of Christianity and the moral laws revealed by God.[3]

One of the most important and most neglected sources of early American political thought is the political sermons preached by Christian ministers upon public occasions such as election days; artillery company ceremonies; Thursday or Fifth Day lectures; days of humiliation, prayer and fasting (in times of hardship); days of thanksgiving (in times of blessing); and other special holidays. These sermons, preached from the earliest days of the colonies until at least the early nineteenth century, were delivered not only in Puritan Massachusetts and New England, but also in the middle colonies, later states, and in the colonies and states of the South. They presented a political theology, a view of history and politics based on the Bible and a Christian theory of natural law, and applied this teaching to the issues of the day. They taught that God is the Creator; that men are fallen in sin; that salvation is attainable only through God's electing grace, via faith in Christ; that God works through personal and collective covenants, affecting individual lives, church communities, and society, giving divine truth and providential direction; and that men ought to live according to the law of liberty revealed in Christ. Even in the eighteenth century they taught that the created world is good, that man is a moral agent who is responsible to live rightly before God, obeying God's laws; that man is by nature free to obey God, living in accordance with what is true and right, or to disobey God, living in accordance with what is false and wrong (and that there are consequences for both kinds of choices). They taught that civil government is necessary to restrain men from evil deeds; that justice is the purpose of civil government, but that civil government may command that which is unjust; that civil government should protect liberty, and that to do so it must be based on the virtue of its rulers and of the people; and that liberty is based on truth and justice stated in the eternal laws made available to man by God.[4]

Christianity and Christian political thought did not cease to be influential during or any time soon after the winning of independence, the framing of our early state constitutions, the framing and ratification of the Articles of Confederation, or the framing and ratification of the Constitution and the Bill of Rights. On the contrary, Christianity remained fundamental to the faith and political thought of the statesmen who gave us these fundamental governmental documents. John Eidsmoe's careful survey of the lives and thought of thirteen of our key early "founders" indicates that eleven of the thirteen were "spiritual descendants of John Calvin" and only Jefferson and, to a lesser extent, Franklin, were "children of the Enlightenment," while all thirteen had "great respect for organized religion, particularly for Christianity."[5]

---

[1] Donald S. Lutz and Charles S. Hyneman, "The Relative Influence of European Political Writers on Late Eighteenth-Century American Political Thought," *American Political Science Review* 189 (1984): 189-197; this study is summarized and discussed in John Eidsmoe, *Christianity and the Constitution: The Faith of Our Founding Fathers* (Grand Rapids: Baker Book House, 1987), 51-53.

[2] Eidsmoe, 72; see also Eidsmoe, 54-73.

[3] See Sandoz, *A Government of Laws*, especially 83-217, which provides an excellent, learned description of the relationship of Christianity to our traditional American political thought.

[4] Sandoz, *Political Sermons of the American Founding Era 1730-1805*, xiv-xxiv.

[5] Eidsmoe, 342; Eidsmoe, 339-342, summarizes the findings of his survey (77-338) of the lives and thought of these thirteen key "founding fathers."

Law, Legal Thought, and Legal Education

Christianity was also basic to early American law, legal thought, and legal education. Early American laws were not perfectly Biblical, but they were dominated by Biblical principles and contained many unmistakable (favorable) references to Christianity.[1] This is seen not only in the laws enacted by state and local governments but also in the common law of England, which was basic to the laws of each of the colonies. A product of the medieval Christian heritage, the common law, a huge mass of judges' decisions beginning in the twelfth century, continuing through the succeeding centuries, and somewhat influenced by Puritanism, was basically and overwhelmingly (though not purely) Christian law, being based on the Bible and a Christian version of natural law. The public wrongs punishable under the common law (as indicated in volume 4 of Blackstone's *Commentaries on the Laws of England*) were obviously based on actions prohibited by the Bible. After independence, the common law was continued as fundamental to the laws of the several states (minus laws supporting the authority of the king, Parliament, the hereditary nobility, and the Anglican Church as the established church). In early America and beyond the Civil War lawyers, legal scholars, and state and federal courts upheld Christian principles of law such as the prohibition of an atheist's testimony and of blasphemy, affirmed that Christianity is basic to the common law and is therefore basic to the laws of the states, and reaffirmed that the laws of the states and the nation are founded upon Christianity.[2] Early American law was based on Biblical law, Christian theories of natural law, and Christianity in the common law.[3]

Early American legal education was based squarely upon English law, and particularly upon the works of Sir Edward Coke and William Blackstone, the great systematizers and commentators on English law and the common law. Coke's *Institutes of the Laws of England* (1628), and particularly its first volume, known as *Coke upon Littleton*, were the second greatest direct influence on colonial and early American lawyers' legal education. Blackstone's

Commentaries on the Laws of England (4 vols., 1765-1769) was the greatest direct influence on the education of early American lawyers and gentlemen through the first half of the nineteenth century. Through the early nineteenth century, the works of Coke were reprinted, seriously studied, and cited as authoritative by American lawyers and judges. Blackstone's *Commentaries* were reprinted, studied and cited even longer.

Both men taught Christian philosophies of law. Coke taught that God writes His eternal moral law, the law of nature, on the hearts of the people as part of the nature of man; that the essence of that law is reason written into the hearts of the people by their Creator; that the common law of England, coming from the people and declared by judges in particular legal cases, is the fundamental law of the state; that the common law is superior to royal prerogative, statutory laws, and all forms of arbitrary power; and that every act of rulers and every judicial case is to be judged by the standard of this ancient, God-given law.[4] Blackstone taught that God taught man His law, the law of nature, shortly after the creation; that because of God's penalty on Adam's sin, man's reason and understanding are fundamentally flawed, yet man still retains a basic knowledge of the law of nature, so men create various flawed theories of "natural law"; that because God is merciful He has revealed His laws to man in the Scriptures of the Old and New Testaments, so that man has a fuller, clearer understanding of God's law available to him in the Bible.[5] Through these two great scholars early Americans received a deeply Christian philosophy of law which pointed them to God-given moral laws available through "nature" and, particularly, the Bible.

Nor did early American lawyers', judges', and scholars' legal thought depart from these influences—despite the propaganda we have been subjected to about "Enlightenment" rationalism ruling early nineteenth century intellectual life. The series of revivals which began in about 1800 and continued throughout the first half of the nineteenth century changed American Christianity, but they did not change American legal thought. Christianity, continued, almost unchallenged, to influence American legal thought as well as the law. American lawyers, judges, and legal scholars, even when they declared that the law was a science, proclaimed that the common law was the same as the divine law available through both reason and revelation. They further maintained that equity is based upon natural law, defended the Christianity of the common law and of the laws of these United States against Jefferson's argument to the contrary and against other legal challenges, maintained that they and the clergy were engaged in a common enterprise, and argued that the truth of Christianity can be solidly established by rational evidence. Even Unitarian judges and legal scholars affirmed the union of Christianity and American law.[6] Thus, early American legal thought resoundingly affirmed the Christianity of the American people of the states and nation, the fundamentally Christian nature of American laws, and specific Christian principles of our laws.

---

[1] See, for example, W. Keith Kavenagh, ed., *Foundations of Colonial America: A Documentary History*, 3 vols.(6 vols. paperback) (New York: Chelsea House, [1974] 1983. Although these are colonial laws, the vast majority of them were continued after independence, for independence did not constitute a radical break with the English legal tradition—the content of the law— except for the abandonment of the authority of the king and Parliament, the hereditary nobility, the Anglican Church as the established church, and laws pertaining thereto.

[2] On the Christianity of the laws of these United States, including judicial decisions, see Jones, "Christianity in the Constitution," 145-230 and passim; David J. Brewer, *The United States: A Christian Nation* (Smyrna, Georgia: The American Vision, [1905] 1996), 14-30; and Steven Alan Samson, "Crossed Swords: Church and State in American History" (Ph.D. Dissertation, University of Oregon, 1984).

[3] Jones, "Christianity in the Constitution," 174-224.

[4] On Coke and his legal philosophy and teaching, see Jones, "Christianity in the Constitution," 162-173.

[5] On Blackstone and his legal teaching and influence, see Jones, "Christianity in the Constitution," 149-162.

[6] See Perry Miller, *The Life of the Mind in America: from the Revolution to the Civil War* (New York: Harcourt, Brace & World, 1965), 99-268, and Jones, "Christianity in the Constitution," 213-221.

Independence

The views fundamental to colonial and early American political and legal thought were basic to the winning of independence.[1] The political thought that undergirded and motivated the colonists' resistance to the tyranny and injustices of George III and Parliament was no mere product of eighteenth century "Enlightenment" rationalism.[2] Rather, it was obviously "religious" thought: Christian thought using elements taken from classical and modern political writers, viewing liberty as no less than a sacred cause, acknowledging God's divine providence and having definite millenarian overtones.[3] The clergy had a prominent role in the resistance and then in the conflict, through their preaching, writing, and leadership.[4] Indeed, so pronounced is the traditional Christian political and legal thought behind the War for Independence that the colonists made it clear that they were fighting for liberty and virtue.[5]

"Religious" issues were, with economic and political ones, basic causes of the American resistance. The prolonged series of religious revivals known as the Great Awakening (beginning in the 1720s and extending into the 1770s, though peaking in the 1730s and 1740s) greatly strengthened Christianity in the colonies and prepared the way for the independence movement.[6] The Episcopal Controversy, the most-debated issue of the colonial period, an attempt of certain Episcopalians in England and America to impose a bishop of the Church of England over all the colonies, was a main cause of the war, for it threatened religious liberty in general, the freedom of the "dissenting" churches to continue to function in America, and the freedom of Episcopalian vestries in the colonies to govern their own churches, as well as foreboding increased taxation of all colonists to support the Church of England.[7]

The teaching of the clergy—particularly the New England clergy, though the same could be seen in the teachings of the clergy of other regions[8]—was also fundamental to the thinking of the American patriots. Alice Baldwin summarized this teaching well:

> God and Christ govern always by fixed rules, by a divine constitution, and therefore so must human rulers. The fundamental constitutions of states may differ; men's rights under

them may be greater or less, but certain great rights are given by Nature and Nature's God to the people. These are a part of every constitution and no ruler is permitted by God to violate them. Rulers cannot change the constitution; that can be done only by the people. But the constitution and the laws must be consonant with divine law. Therefore rulers must study carefully the laws of God, both natural and revealed. In the Bible are founded the maxims and rules of government: there the natural laws are made clearer, there the ruler learns his due authority and its limitations, there the people learn how far they must submit.[9]

American concern for the rule of law and opposition to the arbitrary rule of men was rooted in Christianity and in Christian legal and political thought dating back through the Reformation to the medieval period. That is a chief reason why the "Revolution" could, as Miller said, be "preached to the masses as a religious revival."[10]

Certainly the British recognized the connection between Christianity and the colonists' resistance to king and Parliament. Edmund Burke traced the American resistance precisely to their religious views: to the particular kind of Protestants that early Americans were. The British, who failed to distinguish between Congregationalists and Presbyterians, blamed the conflict on the Presbyterians; consequently, they desecrated and destroyed many Presbyterian churches. Horace Walpole, the British Prime Minister, said, "Cousin America has run off with a Presbyterian parson!" This was a reference to the great Presbyterian educator and leader John Witherspoon.[11]

Christians were leaders of the War for Independence. Ministers were leaders in teaching the Bible's application to civil government, history, and the issues of the day. They preached the "sacred cause of liberty" and urged Americans to fight for both liberty and virtue. Christians of virtually all denominations fought in the war,[12] as did their unconverted neighbors; but the military leaders were predominantly Christians, from George Washington down (Ethan Allen being a notable exception). At the Battle of Yorktown, which effectively ended the war, all but one of the colonels in the colonial army were Presbyterian elders, and more than half of the soldiers and officers of the American army during the Revolution were Presbyterians.[13]

The colonists' political leaders were overwhelmingly Protestant Christians, as is seen in many of the actions of the Continental Congress. Far from behaving like a group of Deists, rationalists, or modern man-centered unbelievers, the Continental Congress, notes Pfeffer:

> [D]id not hesitate to legislate on such subjects as morality, sin, repentance, humiliation, divine service, fasting, prayer, reformation, mourning, public worship, funerals, chaplains, true religion, and Thanksgiving. The Sabbath was recognized to a degree rarely exhibited in other countries; Congress was adjourned and all official business was suspended, as it was on Good Friday.[14]

The proclamations and other state papers of the Continental Congress, moreover:

> ... were replete with references to religion, unabashedly exhibiting a belief in Protestantism. Congress continually evoked, as sanction for its acts, the name of "God," "Almighty God," "Nature's God," "God of Armies," "Lord of Hosts," "His Goodness," "God's Superintending Providence," "Providence of God," "Providence," "Supreme and Universal Providence," "Overruling Providence of God," "Creator of All," "Indulgent Creator," "Great Governor of the World," "The Divinity," "Supreme Disposer of All Events," "Holy Ghost," "Jesus Christ," "Christian Religion," and other expressions of devout Christian Protestantism.[15]

Furthermore, Congress adopted a day of national humiliation, fasting, and prayer; provided chaplains for the army; employed a minister to teach the Indians the principles of Christianity; recommended that the states encourage "religion" (Christianity) and suppress vice; and endorsed an American edition of the Bible. In 1783 Congress concluded a peace treaty with England which was done "In the name of the Most Holy and Undivided Trinity."[16] These actions of the Continental Congress make it clear that that body was a group of Protestant Christians representing their Christian societies and predominantly Christian constituents.

The Declaration of Independence produced by the Second Continental Congress was given the form of a legal plea against the king. Its opening paragraph was an introductory summary of the case against the king, including the theological, philosophical, and legal principles upon which the indictment was based. Its main section was a list of the particular violations of the laws of nature, of nature's God, and of the legal rights of Englishmen which the king (and Parliament) had violated; its concluding paragraph was the closing summary of the plaintiff against the king-in-Parliament. It argued that the king (with the help of Parliament) had violated the laws of nature and of nature's God, the God-given rights which the Creator designs into men; that these violations had been so numerous and systematic that they clearly indicated that the king intended to be a tyrant; and that therefore the American colonists were justified in taking up arms to defend their liberty and to secure their independence. It appealed to God as the Supreme Judge of the world, and explicitly counted on the protection of His divine providence for their colonies' independence and for their own lives, fortunes, and sacred honor.

Moreover, the Declaration was an identifiably Christian document: not a deistic nor a rationalistic one.[17] The legal philosophy behind the Declaration—particularly in its famous opening paragraphs—is easily traceable back through the Reformation (well beyond the eighteenth century Arminian Christian thinker John Locke)[18] to medieval legal and political thought.[19]

---

[1] On the causes and nature of the American "Revolution" (it was a revolution only in the sense of throwing off the rule of the king-in-Parliament, not in the sense of an attempt to overthrow the social, economic, or religious order of American society), see Gary North, ed., *The Journal of Christian Reconstruction*, vol. III, no. 1 (Summer,1976), *Symposium on Christianity and the American Revolution*, and Archie P. Jones, "The Christian Roots of the War for Independence," in 6-51 of that journal.

[2] The notion that eighteenth century European rationalism dominated early American thought from about 1750 on is a myth. See Rousas John Rushdoony, "The Myth of an American Enlightenment," *The Journal of*

Christian Reconstruction, vol. III, no. 1 (Summer, 1976), 69-73.
[3] Sandoz, 134-136, 186, 212-213; Nathan O. Hatch, *The Sacred Cause of Liberty: Republican Thought and the Millennium in Revolutionary New England* (New Haven: Yale University Press, 1977).
[4] Alice M. Baldwin, *The New England Clergy and the American Revolution* (New York: Frederick Ungar Publishing Co., [1928] 1958); Sandoz, *Political Sermons of the American Founding Era*, passim; John Wingate Thornton, *Pulpit of the American Revolution: or, the Political Sermons of the Period of 1776* (Boston: Gould and Lincoln, 1860); J.T. Headley, *Chaplains and Clergy of the Revolution* (Collingswood, New Jersey: Christian Beacon, [1864] 1976).
[5] Marvin Olasky, *Fighting for Liberty and Virtue: Political and Cultural Wars in Eighteenth-Century America* (Wheaton, Illinois: Crossway Books, 1995).
[6] See Alan Heimert, *Religion and the American Mind: From the Great Awakening to the Revolution* (Cambridge: Harvard University Press, 1966).
[7] The classic work on this is Carl Bridenbaugh, *Mitre and Scepter: Transatlantic Faiths, Ideas, Personalities and Politics 1689-1775* (New York: Oxford University Press, 1962).
[8] Sandoz, *Political Sermons of the American Founding Era*, passim.
[9] Baldwin, 35.
[10] Perry Miller, "From the Covenant to the Revival," in Perry Miller, *Nature's Nation* (Cambridge: Harvard University Press, 1967), 110.
[11] Quoted in Boettner, 383, who also provides further evidence, 383-384, of the Presbyterian and Calvinistic basis of the War for Independence.
[12] Mark A. Noll, *Christians in the American Revolution* (Washington, D.C.: Christian University Press, 1977) traces four different responses of Christian denominations to the war: patriotic, reforming, loyalist, and pacifist; he misses the importance of medieval and Reformation Christian legal and political thought and resistance theory—traditional applied Christian theology—in the "Revolution."
[13] Boettner, 384.
[14] Leo Pfeffer, *Church, State, and Freedom* (Boston: Beacon Press, 1953), 107.
[15] Pfeffer, 106-107.
[16] Pfeffer, 107-108.
[17] Jones, "The Christian Roots of the War for Independence," 42-50.
[18] Jones, "The Christian Roots of the War for Independence," 46.
[19] Gary T. Amos, *Defending the Declaration: How the Bible and Christianity Influenced the Writing of the Declaration of Independence* (Brentwood, Tennessee: Wolgemuth & Hyatt, 1989).

Religious Liberty in a Christian Ethical Context

With independence came the beginning of the political battles for religious liberty in the several states. These struggles were motivated by what Americans came to call "the voluntary principle," the freedom of each individual to support the church, denomination, and religious work which he chose to aid, without being coerced to do so. The voluntary principle opposed the traditional concept that an established church or denomination was necessary for a nation or people. An established church required the imposition of tithes or taxes on all, regardless of individual belief, and (among other things) the persecution of individuals and groups considered heretical by the rulers of the church. Most American Protestants believed that in winning these battles they had avoided submitting the church to the civil magistrates' authority and avoided calling upon people to resist civil magistrates who would persecute dissenting churches. The churches prospered with this freedom, a freedom new in the history of the world,[1] so much so that both de Tocqueville and Philip Schaff noted the great strength of Christianity in America. Schaff declared: "The United States are by far the most religious and Christian country in the world; and that, just because religion is there most free."[2]

These battles against state established churches were not struggles for religious liberty in the abstract. Rather, they were efforts to end each state's established church or legal preference for one denomination over all other Christian denominations. They were not efforts to leave all men free to practice any and every religion known to or conceivable by man, for they did not seek to make men free to do things which violate the good order or safety of the state and its people. They did not seek to free men to violate the basic ethical standards of Christianity and thereby to practice license, but to guarantee the liberty of men to worship God in ways consistent with Christian morality.

Christians led the efforts for disestablishment and formed the great mass of public support for the efforts to end legal preference for a given Christian denomination in each state. True, Jefferson was prominent in the legislative effort to disestablish the Anglican Church in Virginia, but where are the "Jeffersons" (unbelievers) in the battles for disestablishment in other states? There are none, or virtually none. But the truth is that Jefferson hid his objections to Biblical Christianity from the public. He publicly supported Christianity, and never came close to establishing a "wall of separation" between Christianity and civil government while he was in public office.[3] Moreover, Jefferson's famous "Bill Establishing Religious Freedom" did not divorce Christianity from Virginia law and was part of a revision of the Virginia legal code in regard to religion which, far from separating Christianity from civil government and law, retained strong ties between Christianity and Virginia law.[4]

In no state did the disestablishment effort feature anti-Christian (or pro-secularist) rhetoric. This is a key indication that those seeking disestablishment did not desire to de-Christianize their state's civil government, laws, or public life. There were no statements that the aim was to remove Christianity from all connections with civil government, law, or the conduct of public life.[5] There were few or no calls for a religiously "neutral" or a secularist civil government or legal order. There were, however, Christian movements against state support of Unitarian unbelief via Unitarian infiltration of Congregational churches in Connecticut and Massachusetts. The rhetoric of the celebrated opponents of established churches—Isaac Backus, John Leland, James Madison, and Samuel Davies—was Christian, not Deistic, rationalist, or unbelieving rhetoric.

Another key indication that the motivation behind the struggles for disestablishment and the achievement of "religious liberty" was not a desire for religious freedom in the abstract is the results of disestablishment. In no state did disestablishment lead to de-Christianization of the civil government, laws, or conduct of public life under the new order. Christianity remained fundamental to the legal orders of the several states long after disestablishment.[6]

All of this indicates that the movements for the establishment of "religious liberty" were neither secularist nor religiously "neutral" (as if one could be neutral in regard to God and "religion"!). Rather, the exercise of "religious liberty" sought by those who brought about disestablishment in the several states was clearly conceived to be consistent with Christian ethics. That is why the states retained laws against blasphemy of God or of any of the persons of the Trinity, laws against atheists' testimony in courts, and laws prohibiting other violations of Christian morality. Even the passage of the First Amendment, in a sense the culmination of the struggles for disestablishment in these United States, was not motivated by a desire to make atheism civilly equal to Christianity. For, as Justice Joseph Story explained in 1835, the purpose of the First Amendment is not to promote or countenance infidelity but rather "to exclude all rivalry among Christian sects [denominations], and to prevent any national ecclesiastical establishment, which should give to a hierarchy the exclusive patronage of the national government."[7]

---

[1] Miller, *The Life of the Mind in America*, 40-43.
[2] Quoted in Miller, *The Life of the Mind in America*, 40.
[3] Archie P. Jones, *Thomas Jefferson: The Man and the Myth* (Marlborough, New Hampshire: Plymouth Rock Foundation, 1998).
[4] On this Daniel L. Dreisbach, "In Pursuit of Religious Freedom: Thomas Jefferson's Church-State Views Revisited," in Luis E. Lugo, ed., *Religion, Public Life, and the American Polity* (Knoxville: University of Tennessee Press, 1993), 74-114, and "A New Perspective on Jefferson's Views on Church-State Relations: The Virginia Statute for Establishing Religious Freedom in Its Legislative Context," *The American Journal of Legal History*, vol. XXXV, no. 2 (April, 1991), 173-204, are must reading.
[5] Baptist minister John Leland came closest to this, yet Leland was not consistent, or overstated his true position regarding the relationship between religion and civil government, for he preached a sermon in the halls of Congress during one of the Sunday worship services held in those halls during Jefferson's administration.
[6] On the struggles for disestablishment in the states and the results thereof, see Jones, "Christianity in the Constitution," 397-459.
[7] Quoted in Miller, *The Life of the Mind in America*, 37.

State Constitutions, Declarations of Rights, and Bills of Rights

With the winning of independence and shortly after, the statesmen of the era framed our early American state constitutions, declarations of rights, and bills of rights.

These were all both republican and Christian. They grew out of the Christian societies of their respective states and out of the Christian legal and political traditions and views of the states' citizens and political leaders. There is no need to claim that the Christianity of the people of these societies was perfect, nor that Christianity was flawlessly expressed in these documents. Imperfection may be conceded, and the clarity and beauty of Christianity's expression varied, but the Christianity of these early governmental documents is unmistakable in their rhetoric and in their principles.

The rhetoric of our early state constitutions was definitely Christian. Their references to God indicate that the men who framed them recognized the nature and authority of God and acknowledged that they, the people of their states, and their states' civil governments are under the authority of God and are dependent upon His divine providence. These documents also manifest a covenantal view of the relationship of God to the people of the state and to their civil government: that they, like Israel of old, are under the rule and authority of God; that they are obligated to maintain faith in Him and so also to obey His moral laws; that without such virtue their liberty will be lost; that Jesus Christ is both Savior and Lord, who rules the universe by His divine providence.

The principles—fundamental laws or truths—conveyed in the rhetoric of these documents are Christian. They show a Christian view of law and rights: that right, rights, and law originate in God, and that civil government is duty-bound to honor God's law and the God-given rights of men. They manifest a Christian view of the nature of man as it relates to civil government: that all men are fallen in sin and yet are possessors of certain God-given rights; that the rulers of civil government, too, are sinful and so liable to abuse their powers; that well-designed civil governments are necessary to protect against the sins of power-hungry men; that civil governments should be limited and constitutional; and that there are rights of resistance against the injustice and tyranny of the rulers of civil government. Christian concern, too, is evident in the Christian qualifications for public office, Christian oaths of office, legal exemptions for pacifist Christians (but, significantly, only Christians), and the encouragement of Christian education. A like concern is evident in the many Christian established or quasi-established church arrangements. Seven states gave legal preference to Christianity or Protestant Christianity. Three had Christian requirements for public office, though they had no established or quasi-established church. New York had "full religious freedom," but with a Protestant test oath for public office and a requirement that naturalized citizens forswear allegiance to all foreign ecclesiastical and civil princes and potentates. Virginia and Rhode Island had "full religious freedom," while also having Christian provisions in their constitutions. Biblical thinking is obvious in these documents' teaching a theme that is common to early American political thought: that virtue is necessary to maintain liberty and that "religion"(in context, Christianity)is necessary to produce the virtue which is essential to preserve liberty.[1]

---

[1] Archie P. Jones, *Christianity and Our State Constitutions, Declarations, and Bills of Rights, Parts I and II* (Marlborough, New Hampshire: Plymouth Rock Foundation, 1993).

The Articles of Confederation

The thinking behind our early state constitutions was similar to that of our first national constitution, the *Articles of Confederation*, for the *Articles* grew out of the same society and legal and political tradition as did the state constitutions. The great majority of the Continental Congress and of the committee which put the *Articles* into its finished form were Christians.

The rhetoric of the *Articles of Confederation* was Christian. The *Articles* contain three references to God. Once it refers to Him as the "Great Governor of the World" who has inclined the hearts of the state legislatures to approve and authorize the states' representatives in the Continental Congress to ratify the *Articles*. Twice (once in the paragraph before Article I and in the last paragraph of the *Articles*) it recognizes the lordship of Jesus Christ in stating, respectively, the date of the agreement of Congress on the *Articles* (1777) and the date of completion of the *Articles* (1778): "in the Year of Our Lord." This is the system of dating historical events which is used in Christian countries. It dates events from the birth of Jesus Christ, whom Christians proclaim to be both the long-awaited Savior and the Lord, the King of Kings and Lord of Lords, who rules sovereignly over heaven and earth. This is consistent with the document's central reference to God as the "Great Governor of the World" (not as a Deistic spectator-"God" who merely observes the world's events), and it makes clear the fact that Jesus Christ is the Lord who governs the world.

The rhetoric of the *Articles* thus teaches the Christian or Biblical principles that Christ is Lord and that He is in a covenantal relationship with the people and the civil government of these United States. This means that He is in authority over these United States, their people, and their civil governments; that they have a special, very serious relationship to Him; that they are obligated to obey Him and His laws; and (among other things) that He will bless them—since He governs history—for faith in Him and obedience to His commandments, or curse or judge them when they depart from faith in Him and from obedience to His law-word.

The *Articles* contain other Biblical principles. The fact that they implicitly recognize the divinity of Christ (as well as His humanity) and His authoritative rule over the people of these United States implies that the civil government must be de-divinized. Since Christ is the Savior, man may not rightly look to civil government or any of its rulers as savior. Since Christ is Lord, His standards of law—of right and wrong, justice and injustice, good and evil—must be the standard for American laws. Otherwise Americans will be in rebellion against Him and so be subject to His just judgments. Civil government may not justly claim God-like, absolute power. Moreover, the *Articles of Confederation* were certainly based upon the Christian premise that all men are sinners and so are liable to abuse political power. From this, too, it follows that the authority and power of civil government must be limited. The *Articles* certainly sought to limit severely the powers and authority of the central government which it established and contained many means by which to do so.

Finally, the rule of law is a concept based upon the very nature of God Himself, for He never changes, so His laws never change. This means that since man's law must conform to God's law, human rulers must conform to God's laws, may not make laws which violate God's holy laws, and may not rule arbitrarily. The *Articles* were certainly designed to encourage the rule of law and to discourage the arbitrary, changeable rule of men, for it implicitly acknowledged the authority of God and explicitly delegated few powers to the central government, made it very difficult to pass a law, and made it extremely difficult to amend the *Articles*.

These were not all the Biblical principles of the *Articles of Confederation*. Christianity is the great religion of representation, and representative civil government has flowed from Christianity. The *Articles* established a cautiously designed representative government to handle the carefully limited concerns of the people of the states. In addition, Christianity is the only worldview which affirms the equal ultimacy of the one (unity) and the many (individuality, or the reality and importance of particular things), for God, being triune, is both one and many. Furthermore, things are one in God, in His creation and providence, and yet each thing which He has created and sustains is real and significant. So politically, Christianity strikes a balance between unity and diversity, central authority and the authority of more localized civil governments, order and individual liberty.[1] This, too, is seen in the *Articles*, which created a central government of very limited powers but reserved authority over their own internal matters to each state government, and which was certainly intended to preserve and protect individual liberty. Finally, the *Articles of Confederation* were designed to protect legally innocent life, private property, liberty, and justice, all of which standards of ethics are easily traceable to the Scriptures.[2]

---

[1] Rushdoony's *The One and the Many* is the best study of this religious and philosophical problem and its implications.

[2] Archie P. Jones, *America's First Covenant: Christian Principles in the Articles of Confederation* (Marlborough, New Hampshire: Plymouth Rock Foundation, 1993).

The Constitution and the Bill of Rights

Our early state constitutions and the *Articles of Confederation* were precedents for the Constitution of these United States, and the state constitutions were the historical and legal context of the Constitution. While the Constitution was developed because of certain shortcomings in the design of the *Articles* and of the state constitutions, the Constitution did not represent an abandonment of the fundamental Christian thinking which undergirded the *Articles* and the state constitutions, declarations, and bills of rights. Similarly, while the Bill of Rights was fashioned because many Americans saw (or, to put it mildly, thought they saw) defects in the Constitution, the Bill of Rights did not constitute an abandonment of the Christian view of God, men, law, and politics upon which the Constitution was framed. In fact, the Bill of Rights was added to the Constitution precisely to calm the fears of those whose distrust of the sinful nature of man was, like the views of the framers of the *Articles*, greater than that of the Federalists who supported ratification of the Constitution to replace the *Articles of Confederation*.

Contrary to what we have been told for so long, the religious views of the statesmen who wrote the Constitution and the Bill of Rights indicate that they had no desire to be "neutral" among all the religions of man; nor did they desire to foist a secularist fundamental law upon the overwhelmingly Christian, Protestant people of these United States. Professor M.E. Bradford's careful, thorough research into the lives of the framers and ratifiers of the U.S. Constitution indicates that at least 51 and as many as 53 of the 55 framers of the Constitution, and a similar percentage of the leading men in the state ratification conventions which decided whether to adopt the Constitution, were (from all that the written records of their lives can tell us) orthodox Christians, not Deists, rationalists, or any other sort of unbelievers.[1] The fact that the framers and ratifiers were neither pietists, nor intellectual schizophrenics, but, rather, traditional Christians, indicates an intention to have the Constitution conform to traditional American thinking about civil government and law and an intention to make the document consistent with the political and legal implications of the Christianity they professed.

Like the state constitutions, declarations, and bills of rights and the *Articles of Confederation*, the Constitution contains some Christian rhetoric and many Biblical or Christian principles or truths.[2]

Although the Constitution does not contain as many references to God as does the *Articles*, it does contain two implicit references to Christianity. The first (in Article I, Section 7) excludes Sunday--the Christian Sabbath—as a day on which presidential votes could be counted. This excluded Sunday as a day for normal work, a Biblical precept recognized by Christians throughout the world and particularly honored by Calvinists. The second (in Article VII) states that the Constitution was "Done . . . in the year of our Lord [1787]" and is the same kind of traditional Christian designation of time found in the *Articles of Confederation*.

This reference to "the year of our Lord" refutes the common error (made by friends,[3] as well as by opponents,[4] of the idea that Christianity underlies and/or permeates the Constitution) of the unhappily common belief that the Constitution nowhere mentions God or Christ.[5] Given a basic understanding of Christian theology, the plain implications of the reference are the same as those of the similar references in the *Articles of Confederation* (or anywhere else!): The Bible is true. Christ is the Savior. Christ, risen from the grave, ascended into heaven, and seated at the right hand of God the Father, is also the Lord, the sovereign Ruler of heaven and earth. The people of these United States are under the authority of Christ, whom they collectively acknowledge to be Lord. They have a special, covenantal relationship to Him, and that relationship, premised on His providential intervention in and rule of history, involves His blessings on the nation which has faith in Him and keeps His commandments, and curses on the nation which collectively turns from faith in Him and so violates His holy laws. Hence, the nation must look to Him, and it and its civil governments must obey His laws.[6]

The officials of the civil governments of these United States, under the Constitution, were also required to look to God in swearing or affirming their oaths of office. It was common knowledge in America when the Constitution was framed and ratified that an oath or affirmation is a solemn religious act made to God, not merely to the people. It involved an appeal to more than human authority and to a set of sanctions that are greater than mere human institutions can impose, and therefore entailed a sense of religious obligation. In swearing (or affirming) to support the Constitution, therefore, public officials are making a solemn promise before none less than God. Furthermore, in swearing to support the Constitution they are affirming to uphold a Christian constitution that acknowledges the lordship of Christ.[7]

Article VI of the Constitution does prohibit a religious test for federal government office, but this was the product of a desire to avoid the evils of a national established church, not of a wish to establish either a religiously "neutral" or a secularist fundamental law. This provision was proposed and seconded by Christian statesmen. When the clause was debated in the state ratification conventions, the debates were conducted as discussions among Christians, not as arguments between unbelievers and Christians. The arguments for the prohibition of a religious test were sometimes made by ministers and were based on such Biblical concerns that evil men will lie about their religious beliefs in order to get public office; that Christianity has flourished much more when it has not been advanced by the power of an established church backed by the state; and that a dictatorial spirit, religious persecutions, and religious wars result from a national established church.[8]

Beyond this, the Constitution contains other Biblical principles: the de-divinized state, or limited government; many carefully considered protections against the sinful nature of all men (though not as many as the authors of the *Articles of Confederation* or the prescient Antifederalist opponents of the Constitution thought requisite); establishing justice (a justice, given the Christian context of the Constitution in American law and legal thought, the Christian views of the framers and ratifiers, and the document's own recognition of the lordship of Christ, understood in Christian terms); ensuring domestic tranquility; provision for the common defense; promoting the general welfare (not via allowing the officials of the central government to do whatever they wish in the name of "the general welfare" nor via socialistic legalized theft!); and securing the blessings of liberty for present and future generations.[9]

---

[1] M.E. Bradford, *Religion and the Framers: The Biographical Evidence* (Marlborough, New Hampshire: Plymouth Rock Foundation, 1991) and *A Worthy Company: Brief Lives of the Framers of the United States Constitution* (Marlborough, New Hampshire: Plymouth Rock Foundation, 1982). The former work summarizes a much larger body of evidence concerning the Christianity of the Framers, as Dr. Bradford indicated on page 25, note 1 of *Religion and the Framers*. See also Eidsmoe, 77-342.

[2] For brief discussions of some of these, see Eidsmoe, 355-378 and Archie P. Jones, *Christian Principles in the Constitution and the Bill of Rights, Parts I and II* (Marlborough, New Hampshire: Plymouth Rock Foundation, 1994); the summary which follows is taken from the latter.

[3] For example, Isaac Cornelison, *The Relation of Religion to Civil Government in the United States* (New York: DaCapo Press, [1895] 1970) and Sanford H. Cobb, *The Rise of Religious Liberty in the United States: A History* (New York: Johnson Reprint Corporation, [1902] 1970).

[4] For example, secularist theorist/propagandist Leonard Levy, *The Establishment Clause* (New York: Macmillan, 1986) and "civil religion" theorists Robert N. Bellah and Phillip E. Hammond, *Varieties of Civil Religion* (San Francisco: Harper and Row, 1980).

[5] Jones, "Christianity in the Constitution," 231-287, provides an extended discussion of the subject and maintains that the Constitution is not silent about God but rather affirms—by clear implication—the lordship of Christ.

[6] Jones, *Christian Principles in the Constitution and the Bill of Rights, Part I*, 14-17, "Christianity in the Constitution," 257-264, and Archie P. Jones, "The Myth of Political Polytheism," originally published by the Plymouth Rock Foundation, reprinted in *The Journal of Christian Reconstruction, Symposium on Reconstruction in Church and State*, vol. XIV, no.1 (Fall, 1996), 279-282, discusses the implications of this clause more fully.

[7] Jones, *Christian Principles in the Constitution and the Bill of Rights, Part I*, 17-19.

[8] Jones, "Christianity in the Constitution," 288-338, and *Christian Principles in the Constitution and the Bill of Rights, Part I*, 19-22; see also Jones, "The Myth of Political Polytheism," 282-286. A more or

less easily accessible primary source is an article by one of the Framers of the Constitution, Oliver Ellsworth, "On a Religious Test for Holding Public Office," in *The Annals of America*, vol. 3, *1784-1796: Organizing the New Nation* (Chicago, London, etc.: Encyclopaedia Britannica, Inc. 1968), 169-172.

[9] Jones, *Christian Principles in the Constitution and the Bill of Rights, Parts I and II*.

A Tradition of Christian Civil Government and Law

Until at least the middle of the twentieth century, these United States had a strong tradition of the union of Christianity and American civil government, law, and public life at the national as well as the state and local levels of government. In the twentieth century, modern man's rebellion against God, the Bible, and Christianity led to a deliberate distortion of the intentions behind the First Amendment so as to exclude Christianity from American civil government, law, and public life.[1] The historical record and the logic of the debates on what became the First Amendment in the First Congress make it clear that the First Amendment was not intended to de-Christianize American civil government, law, or public life.[2] Rather, the First Amendment was intended to prevent the creation of a national established church like the Church of England; to leave people free to exercise their religious beliefs, so long as those beliefs did not yield conduct contrary to Christian ethics; and to use freedom of speech, freedom of the press, and freedom of assembly to influence the working of civil government.[3]

Of course, until the U.S. Supreme Court's majority of humanistic "liberals" began in effect rewriting the First Amendment, and rewriting the Fourteenth Amendment to make it "incorporate" the Bill of Rights (and so the First Amendment), and apply the Bill of Rights to the states, there were many, many kinds of connections between Christianity and the states' governments, and Christianity was fundamental to the laws of the several states. But there were also many kinds of connections between Christianity and the functioning of the federal government, and many of these continue even today.[4]

Leaving aside consideration of Christian ethics as fundamental to the laws enacted by the central government (a subject too lengthy to include here but one which would yield a great body of evidence in support of the thesis that Christian ethics were fundamental to "federal" law), a survey of the kinds of connections between Christianity and our national government, law, and public life makes it clear that neither our early statesmen nor their successors in Congress, the White House, or the Federal Courts intended to separate Christianity from our law or public life.

The actions of the very First Congress testify to this, for that Congress made a divine service part of President Washington's inauguration, provided chaplains for each house of Congress, and established a system of military chaplains. It also reenacted the *Northwest Territories Ordinance of 1787*, which provided that federal land be set aside for schools to promote "religion, morality, and knowledge." After debating what became the First Amendment, that Congress debated whether to grant exemption from military duty to Quakers and members of other *Christian* pacifist denominations—and not to anyone else. On the day after it completed its work on what would become the First Amendment, that Congress called upon President Washington to proclaim a national day of public thanksgiving and prayer to God.

Presidential inaugural addresses also manifest a connection between Christianity and our central government, for in these official addresses our presidents routinely refer respectfully to God or to His divine providence and to the nation's and president's dependence upon Him. This clearly implies a covenantal relationship between God and these United States, teaches that if we obey God's laws the nation will be blessed, and presents national difficulties as the consequence of sins and God's chastisement, not merely the result of human or naturalistic factors. Presidential annual addresses and special messages to Congress (and thence to the American public) conveyed the same view of the relationship between God and our civil government and history.

As indicated above, presidential and other oaths of office, sworn in accordance with the Constitution, testify to Christianity in two ways: (1) they are understood to be religious acts before God, and (2) they are in fact solemn promises to uphold a Constitution which, by clear implication, recognized the lordship of Christ.

Presidential proclamations of days of humiliation, fasting, and prayer, or of days of thanksgiving, similarly testify to the continuing connection between Christianity and our national government. Furthermore, these do so with the authority of both the President and Congress, for they were declared by presidents upon the request of Congress.

The actions of presidents like Thomas Jefferson and James Madison witness to the continuing power of our tradition of connections between Christianity and our national government, even though both men are customarily and propagandistically presented to us as men who advocated either a strict "religious neutrality" or a secularist "absolute separation" between "church and state" (that is: Christianity and civil government). Neither of these presidents actually divorced Christianity from civil government when he was in public office or when he was president.

President Jefferson made neither Thanksgiving Day proclamations nor proclamations of days of prayer. He did write his famous letter to the Danbury Baptist Association, in which he spoke of "a wall of separation between church and state," but he did not in fact separate Christianity from his conduct of the national government as President. In his inaugural addresses and annual messages to Congress, Jefferson refers to God in ways that Christians could accept, says that he believes in the usefulness of prayer, declares that it is a duty to praise God as the Author of all mercies, uses Biblical symbolism which likens God's relationship to these United States to His covenantal relationship to ancient Israel, and praises the Christian religion of the people of these United States. While he was President, the Washington, D.C. schools, in keeping with his plan, used the Bible and Isaac Watts' great Protestant *Hymnal* as textbooks. Jefferson recommended and signed treaties with several Indian tribes who used federal government money to support various Christian purposes and signed into law Congressional acts which helped spread Christianity among the Indians. He also participated in Christian worship services that were held in the chambers of Congress during his administration.[5]

President Madison, who was a congressman in the First Congress, had helped formulate the legislation for systems of congressional chaplains and military chaplains. At the request of Congress, he made four proclamations of national days of thanksgiving to God. His inaugural and other addresses fit well into the covenantal pattern of early American presidential addresses. Like Jefferson, as President he frequently attended the Christian worship services held in the halls of Congress.

The system of congressional chaplains and the system of military chaplains constitute other unmistakable connections between Christianity and our national government, law, and public life.

The early American practice of Congress was to have the halls of Congress used for Christian worship services on Sunday, the Christian Sabbath. The chaplains of Congress or ministers invited by them preached in these services. The U. S. Marine Corps Band, in full dress uniform, played the Psalms and hymns that were sung by government officials and others attending these worship services.

As has been intimated in the case of President Jefferson, the treaties approved by the central government with Indian tribes and others frequently show national government support of Christianity. Many of these treaties were negotiated with active participation of the President; all of them had to be approved by at least two-thirds of the Senate. Many of these treaties recognized God in the designation of their date: "the year of our Lord . . ." or "A.D." (*Anno Domini*, the year of our Lord). Many others provided for the payment of national government money to support or spread Christianity among the Indians.

For many decades—until 1896—the national government gave support to the advancement of Christianity among the Indians by supporting Christian missionaries, schools, and religious teaching among the Indians. The purpose was to Christianize and civilize the Indians. Congresses and presidents cooperated in these endeavors.

Concerning national government support of Christian education, it was not only the First Congress which reenacted the *Northwest Ordinance of 1787* and thereby paid "federal government" money to support religion, morality, and education by way of setting aside land to be used to support schools. Other early American Congresses reenacted the once-famous ordinance each time a new territory in the Old Northwest (now the Midwest) was being readied to come into the Union as a state. Similar actions were taken for states in the Old Southwest (now the Southeast).

The continuing connection between Christianity and our national government are seen, too, in the ceremonies dedicating our national Capital, the District of Columbia, and various "federal government" buildings in it. These sometimes contained both Masonic and Christian ceremonies, but the addresses delivered at these ceremonies were Christian, not religiously neutral.

Completed national government buildings frequently contained Christian signs and symbols, another inescapable evidence of the open acknowledgement of Christianity by our national government.

Even the traditional prayer that opens each session of the U. S. Supreme Court testifies to Christianity, for it calls upon God to "save the United States and this Honorable Court!" Lest the Supreme Court or anyone else suppose that this traditional chant refers to "God" in the abstract, the Christian and Biblical context can easily be established by looking at the copy of the Ten Commandments which hangs, literally, behind and over the heads of the Supreme Court justices.

Christianity has also been recognized traditionally by federal and state courts. This was done by the acceptance of the common law and equity in federal courts. The common law was taught and known to be fundamentally Christian law, and equity, by which the moral code of a people becomes part of the law, was, in Protestant Christian America, deemed to be consistent with Christian ethics. The Bible and a Christian theory (or theories) of natural law were basic to both the common law and equity.

Before the U.S. Supreme Court began to overthrow our traditional jurisprudence regarding "church and state" in 1947, federal judges' decisions repeatedly reaffirmed the Christianity of the American people and their laws. Among these decisions, two cases are particularly noteworthy. In the Mormon Polygamy Cases (1878) the Supreme Court forbade polygamy (a religiously based Mormon practice) because it is contrary to Christian morality. In *Rector, etc., of Holy Trinity Church v. United States* (1892), a unanimous Supreme Court said that a church may contract with a foreign priest or minister to be its pastor even though federal immigration law forbids contracting with foreigners to come here to work because "no purpose of action against religion can be imputed to any legislation, state or national, because this is a religious people." Having surveyed a mass of evidence like that sketched above, Justice Brewer, speaking for the Court, said, "this is a Christian nation."[6]

This great tradition of connections between Christianity and our national and state governments and laws was so strong that when the National Liberal League—a spiritual if not a literal ancestor of the infamous American Civil Liberties Union—attacked support of Christianity by our national and state governments in the early 1870s, it had to demand a virtual revolution in our laws and in the conduct of our civil governments.[7]

---

[1] See David Barton, *The Myth of Separation: What Is the Correct Relationship between Church and State?: An Examination of the Supreme Court's Own Decisions* (Aledo, Texas: Wallbuilder Press, 1989).

[2] See Eidsmoe; Barton; Samson; Cobb; Cornelison; Morris; Jones, "Christianity in the Constitution"; Chester James Antieau, Arthur T. Downey, and Edward C. Roberts, *Freedom from Federal Establishment: Formation and Early History of the First Amendment's Religion Clauses* (Milwaukee: Bruce Publishing Co., 1964); Robert L. Cord, *Separation of Church and State: Historical Fact and Current Fiction* (New York: Lambeth Press, 1982); Norman DeJonge and Jack Van Der Slik, *Separation of Church and State: The Myth Revisited* (Jordan Station, Ontario: Paideia Press, 1985); Daniel L. Dreisbach, *Real Threat and Mere Shadow: Religious Liberty and the First Amendment* (Westchester, Illinois: Crossway Books, 1987); Tim LaHaye, *Faith of Our Founding Fathers* (Brentwood, Tennessee: Wolgemuth & Hyatt, 1987); James McClellan, "The Making and Unmaking of the Establishment Clause," in McGuigan and Rader, eds., *A Blueprint for Judicial Reform* (Washington, D.C.: Free Congress Research and Education Foundation, 1981), 295-324; John W. Whitehead, *The Separation Illusion: A Lawyer Examines the First Amendment* (Milford, Michigan: Mott Media, 1977); R. Kemp Morton, *God in the Constitution* (Nashville: Cokesbury Press, 1933); A. James Reichley, *Religion in American Public Life* (Washington, D.C.: The Brookings Institution, 1985); Mark de Wolfe Howe, *The Garden and the Wilderness: Religion and Government in American Constitutional History* (Chicago: University of Chicago Press, 1965); and Anson Phelps Stokes, *Church and State in the United States*, 3 vols. (New York: Harper and Brothers, 1950).

[3] This is the thesis of Jones, "Christianity in the Constitution," though it is implicitly the thesis of all of the works cited in note 143—even that of Stokes, for the evidence he presents of the connections between Christianity and civil government contradicts his explicit thesis and proves this thesis.

[4] The evidence summarized in the following paragraphs is taken from the corresponding sections in Jones, "Christianity in the Constitution," 654-734, and Jones, *Church and State: The Federal Record* (Marlborough, New Hampshire: Plymouth Rock Foundation, 1994), 7-50.

[5] For a fuller discussion of Jefferson's views and actions regarding "church and state," see Jones, *Thomas Jefferson: The Man and the Myth*.

[6] Quoted in Jones, *Church and State: The Federal Record*, 49. For the whole opinion, see Brewer, 75-89; for the basic evidence upon which the opinion is founded, see Brewer, 14-32.

[7] The program of the National Liberal League is listed and discussed in Jones, *Church and State: The Federal Record*, 50-52.

☐ YES!

I want to receive the Chalcedon Report, as well as information on Chalcedon's other publications.

(The Report is sent by request without charge. However, a tax-deductible donation to cover our costs is requested.)

CHALCEDON *Report*

Name _____ E-mail _____

Address _____

City _____ State _____ Zip _____

Daytime Phone _____ Amount Enclosed _____

☐ Visa   ☐ M/C   ☐ Check   Account Number: _____

Signature _____ Card Exp. Date _____

POSTCARD RATE POSTAGE REQUIRED

CHALCEDON
Report
P.O. Box 158
Vallecito, CA 95251-9989

Charity and Welfare

The basically Biblical view of the nature of man and of the proper, limited duties of civil government which underlay our constitutions and bills of rights meant that civil government was to promote the general welfare of the whole people, and not engage in schemes for the restructuring of society or in legalized theft in order to provide "welfare" for selected groups of people. The carefully limited role of civil government in general and of the central or national government in particular under the Constitution was intended to leave the American people free to do what the Bible tells men to do: provide charity and help to the truly needy.

Until the advent of the modern unconstitutional "welfare state" in the twentieth century, Protestants, Roman Catholics, and Jews all provided effective charity to the needy in these United States via individual and institutional aid that was motivated by Biblical teaching and voluntarily chosen by its providers. Such aid was based upon a Biblical model of compassion which centered around at least seven Biblical principles or standards by which help was to be given to the poor: 1) affiliation with the family and relatives; 2) bonding between the charity volunteers and those whom they were helping; 3) careful categorization of would-be recipients of aid, including a test of the able-bodied's willingness to work; 4) discernment about the spiritual and moral state of each recipient by those providing the aid, combined with discernment in the provision of help; 5) employment, centering on teaching the recipient how to provide for himself or herself and his or her dependents; 6) freedom, focused on showing the aid recipient how to be free of dependence upon the charity from which he or she was getting aid—and certainly upon civil government-provided largesse; and, most important, 7) God, whose existence and attributes are the foundation of hope in this life and in the next for all who believe on Him and whose word and example were the foundation for the vast majority of American charitable activities. With the Roosevelt "New Deal" and particularly with Johnson's "Great Society," virtually every one of these Biblical principles were abandoned, with the predictable consequences that civil government-provided "welfare" became destructive to most of its recipients, worsened the conditions it had allegedly been established to alleviate or eliminate, increased the breakup of the family, and produced greater poverty, crime, and misery.[1]

---

[1] Marvin Olasky, *The Tragedy of American Compassion* (Washington, D.C.: Regnery Publishing, Inc., 1992). As is the case with most of the left wing "crusades," programs, and plans of our times, the attempt to wage "war" on poverty in America was launched to the accompaniment of crisis rhetoric, when conditions of the poor had actually been improving, and the plans and programs of those who claimed to be their benefactors actually made the plight of the poor far worse. See Thomas Sowell, *The Vision of the Anointed* (Basic Books, 1995), 8-30, especially 9-15.

Benevolence and Missions

The voluntary principle so basic to American religious and charitable activity was also fundamental to the ideas of benevolence and missionary activity which came to characterize early American Christianity. As civilized societies transplanted in the wilderness, threatened on their frontiers by surprise attacks from savages (who were often induced to attack by agents of England's national enemies), and then preoccupied with winning independence, the colonists and early Americans devoted most of their religious energies to their own communities and societies. There was plenty of sin to deal with in the colonies, and the Indians' conduct during their raids did not endear them to the colonists or to early Americans.[1] While evangelization of the Indians was basic to the purposes of the colonies, the Church of England did not devote the resources to that enterprise that it later devoted to Africa; and the "dissenting sects" which composed most of Christianity in America had no resources comparable to those of the Roman Catholic Church to devote to missions. Most early Americans were too preoccupied with pioneering, economic activities, and political events to pay much attention to missions.

Still, there were notable, even heroic efforts to evangelize the Indians. The Puritans did more than any other group to evangelize the Indians. John Eliot (1632-1690), the Puritan "Apostle to the Indians," and perhaps our greatest missionary, labored among the Algonquian Indians of Massachusetts for more than fifty years. He sought to Christianize the entire Indian population, to teach them the whole counsel of God and how to apply the Bible to their lives as well as to convert them. Most of the New England clergy were sympathetic to his labors, though many laymen were doubtful about the project. He established fourteen "Praying Indian" towns based on Biblical law, established Christian schools, trained native teachers, and translated the Bible and several Christian books into Algonquian. He had the Indians taught trades and launched businesses so that they could fit into the colonial economy. He gave them all the aid he could during the disastrous King Philip's War (1676). The Thomas Mayhew family worked with John Eliot, evangelizing and teaching the Indians on Martha's

Vineyard, and were blessed with many more conversions than was Eliot. Before the pagan Indians tried to wipe out the English in King Philip's War, English missionaries labored all over New England to convert the savages.[2] The great theologian Jonathan Edwards served as a missionary to the Stockbridge Indians. David Brainerd (1718-1747), the son-in-law of Jonathan Edwards, died at the age of twenty-nine because of overwork and disease acquired while attempting to bring the Gospel to the Indians along the Delaware River. So powerful was Brainerd's desire to reach the heathen for Christ, as conveyed in his *Diary* that was published by his father-in-law after his death, that it has influenced countless Americans and Europeans go to the mission field and stay in that field to advance the cause of Christ.[3]

After independence had been achieved and defended, the new United States was on a sound economic footing. The Indian threat had been well nigh eliminated on the frontier and American Christians were in a better situation to think about missions. During the revivals of the early to mid-nineteenth century the missionary impulse received new life and great impetus. Home missions were emphasized first, then foreign missions. The great motive was to make the nation a distinctly Christian land that would evangelize the heathen nations and peoples of the world, using both its example as a righteous society and its wealth.

A secondary motive was to make America the bulwark of Protestantism. When the heathen frontier in America was Christianized, America would become a missionary nation reaching out to evangelize the world. The whole was driven by the postmillennial hope of Christianity being triumphant in reclaiming the world by converting it to Christ.[4] This belief that the church would be victorious over the forces of Satan in history was a legacy of the historic Calvinism, particularly in the Puritans, many American Christians before the War for Independence, and Northern and Southern Presbyterians.[5] The aim for home and foreign missions was conversion and the moral elevation of the human race. "The blaze of missionary passion in early nineteenth-century America, together with the voluntary principle," says Miller, "made this epoch something unprecedeSnted in Christian history."[6]

[1] For example, Perry Miller, *Errand into the Wilderness* (Cambridge and London: Harvard University Press, [1956] 1978), says that the Indians' 1622 massacre of many of the inhabitants of the Virginia Colony killed the missionary impulse in Virginia. Almost the same could be said of the effect of the devastations of the Indian-initiated King Philip's War (1676) on the English of New England.

[2] Ola Elizabeth Winslow, *John Eliot: "Apostle to the Indians"* (Boston: Houghton Mifflin Co., 1968).

[3] See Oswald J. Smith, *David Brainerd: His Message for Today* (Edinburgh: Marshall, Morgan, and Scott: [1949] 1963). Many editions of David Brainerd's *Diary*—which was written only for his own private use—have been published; one such edition is Jonathan Edwards, ed., *The Life and Diary of David Brainerd* (Chicago: Moody Press, n.d.).

[4] Miller, *The Life of the Mind in America*, 49-58; Miller does not use the term "postmillennial," but postmillennialism is the only eschatology consistent with such a hope; for a summary of the four basic positions on the millennium, see Gary North, *Backward, Christian Soldiers?: An Action Manual for Christian Reconstruction* (Tyler, Texas: Institute for Christian Economics, 1984), 269-271; Greg L. Bahnsen, "The Prima Facie Acceptability of Postmillennialism," *The Journal of Christian Reconstruction*, vol. III, no. 2 (Winter, 1976-1977), 60-68; J. M. Clouse, ed., *The Millennium: Four Views* (Wheaton, Illinois: Intervarsity Press, 1986). Bahnsen, 98-99, notes that postmillennialism provided a great stimulus to American missions, beginning in the early 1800s, and provides a brief summary of the evidence for this. For an introduction to postmillennialism, see Gary North, ed., *The Journal of Christian Reconstruction*, vol. III, no. 2 (Winter, 1976-1977), 1-127; Loraine Boettner, *The Millennium* (Philadelphia: Presbyterian and Reformed Publishing Co., [1957] 1974); J. Marcellus Kik, *An Eschatology of Victory* (Philadelphia: Presbyterian and Reformed Publishing Co., 1971).

[5] On postmillennialism in English and early American history, see Iain H. Murray, *The Puritan Hope: A Study in Revival and the Interpretation of Prophecy* (London: The Banner of Truth Trust, 1971); J.A. DeJonge, *As the Waters Cover the Sea: Millennial Expectations and the Rise of Anglo-American Missions 1640-1810* (Kampen: J.H. Kok, 1970); Bahnsen, 68-104; James B. Jordan, "A Survey of Southern Presbyterian Millennial Views Before 1930," *The Journal of Christian Reconstruction*, vol. III, no. 2 (Winter, 1976-1977), 106-121.

[6] Miller, *The Life of the Mind in America*, 49.

A Great Heritage

The impact of historic Christianity on early America was deep, predominant, and more widespread than the evidence sketched in this work indicates. More evidence of Christianity's influence upon early America can be seen in the Biblical and Christian names (in Spanish and in English) of cities, towns, and places. It can be seen in the evangelization of many of the slaves who formed so considerable and important a portion of early Americans. It can be seen in the fundamental principles and much of the way Americans conducted their business and economic life and in the large degree of economic freedom which early Americans enjoyed and which enabled them to achieve individual, familial, and national economic progress and prosperity which has become legendary and has attracted tens of millions to our shores. Further evidence is seen in the influence of the Bible upon American politics and political rhetoric[1] and on social reform movements.[2]

Not every impact of each branch or movement of Christian thought or action in early America was good. Revivalism, for example, came to dominate Bible-believing Protestant Christianity in these United States. Revivalism, by and large, was a turning from Calvinism to Arminianism, from the conveying of Biblical thought to the manipulation of emotions. The revivals of the nineteenth century accelerated the growth of Arminianism and made it predominant. Arminianism pragmatically concerned itself with preaching, turned self-consciously against traditional learned Protestant theology, and became anti-intellectual.[3] This represented a retreat from serious thought and rendered American Christians less able to defend the Faith and made Christianity less respectable among the educated because it surrendered most areas of thought to non-Christians. It also was a retreat from the whole counsel of God, from the application of the Bible to all areas of thought and life, and from the mainstream of the early American Christian heritage.

Similarly, pietism narrowed the scope of "religion" from the comprehensive concern that the Bible presents to the individual's personal, nearly private relationship with God, an error which renders Christians indisposed to seek to fulfill the Creation Mandate to have dominion over all of life (*Gen. 1: 26-28*), Jesus' mandate that His disciples be salt and light to the world (*Mt. 5:13-16*), His admonitions concerning the continuing validity of His law, God's law (*Mt. 5:17-19*), and the Great Commission of believers to disciple the nations (*Mt. 28:18-20*).

Sin mars every human endeavor, including all the works of Christians, in America and everywhere else. Analysis of every activity done by Christians, much less every activity done in the name of Christianity in early America, and of the extent to which each was Biblical, consistent, and so forth, is far too complicated to be done here. What should be clear is that early America was founded upon the deep, extensive influence of historic Christianity on Western, particularly English or British thought and culture. Early American society, culture, and thought were founded upon the historic Christianity inherited from the medieval period and the Protestant Reformation. That heritage was and is a priceless heritage. It is a heritage that is made greater by the fact that it was not limited to the narrow confines of the personal life of the individual, nor to the ecclesiastical structure and matters of the churches of these United States. It is a great heritage because the depth and scope of Christian influence reached beyond religion in the narrow sense in which most Americans today are accustomed to think of religion.

The impact of historic Christianity gave early Americans a great Christian heritage because it positively and predominantly (though not perfectly) shaped culture, education, science, literature, legal thought, legal education, and political thought. It shaped the fundamental laws of several states and of the nation, the conduct of political life (or at least much of it), the provision for charity, and the launching of missions to the unsaved individuals and peoples within these United States and in foreign lands.

Early Americans, led by Christians, used to recognize that they, as a people, had a relationship to God like that of the ancient Israelites. They saw their society and civil government as being responsible to God and accountable to Him in history for their faith and actions, for they knew that He had made them a Christian nation. Here, as in ancient Israel, God certainly worked with sinners, and American history has not been without many sins and certain times of apostasy. Yet the three Persons of the Trinity have done great things in this land and through God's people. God, not the people of this land, deserves the glory for the great Christian heritage which He, through the work of His people down the centuries, has given to Americans in general and American Christians in particular.

Americans, like nations and peoples everywhere, still are under His authority and rule. We are still responsible to have faith in Him and to obey His commandments. The greatness of America is directly traceable to the great Christian heritage of early Americans. The unequaled blessings that Americans have enjoyed are the fruits of that God-given heritage. The things that threaten those blessings are directly traceable to Americans' later abandonment of the full-orbed Christianity which produced the great Christian heritage of early America.

Americans have a deep obligation to God, to their loved ones and neighbors, and to their posterity to turn back to God and to the whole counsel of God revealed in the Scriptures, to rediscover and recover their great Christian heritage, to maintain that heritage, and to improve upon it for their good and for His glory.

---

[1] James Turner Johnson, ed., *The Bible in American Law, Politics, and Political Rhetoric* (Philadelphia: Fortress Press; Chico, California: Scholars Press, 1985).

[2] Ernest R. Sandeen, ed., *The Bible and Social Reform* (Philadelphia: Fortress Press; Chico, California: Scholars Press, 1982).

[3] Miller, *The Life of the Mind in America*, 59-64.

CHALCEDON CONTEMPORARY ISSUES SERIES
Andrew Sandlin, General Editor

Also in this series:

The Future of the Conservative Movement:
A Chalcedon Symposium

The Late Great GOP and the Coming Realignment
by Colonel V. Doner

The Author

Archie P. Jones has a masters degree in American Studies and a Diplomate in Collegiate Teaching from the University of Miami (Florida) and a Ph.D. in Politics from the University of Dallas. His dissertation "Christianity in the Constitution: The Intended Meaning of the Religion Clauses of the First Amendment," refutes notions that the First Amendment was intended to render our national government, law, or public life neutral among all the religions of man or secularist. He is the author of *Christianity and Our State Constitutions, Declarations of Rights, and Bills of Rights, Parts I and II, America's First Covenant: Christian Principles in the Articles of Confederation, Christian Principles in the Constitution and the Bill of Rights, Parts I and II, Church and State: The Federal Record*, and *Thomas Jefferson: The Myth and the Man*.

Dr. Jones has taught at Texas A&M, Grove City College, and two Christian schools. He currently teaches at Rocky Bayou Christian School, Niceville, Florida, and is an adjunct instructor at Embry-Riddle Aeronautical University and a senior adjunct professor at Saint Leo College.

The Ministry of Chalcedon

CHALCEDON (kal•see•don) is a Christian educational organization devoted exclusively to research, publishing, and to cogent communication of a distinctively Christian scholarship to the world at large. It makes available a variety of services and programs, all geared to the needs of interested ministers, scholars and laymen who understand the propositions that Jesus Christ speaks to the mind as well as the heart, and that his claims extend beyond the narrow confines of the various institutional churches. We exist in order to support the efforts of all orthodox denominations and churches. Chalcedon derives its name from the great ecclesiastical Council of Chalcedon (A.D. 451), which produced the crucial Christological definition: "Therefore, following the holy Fathers, we all with one accord teach men to acknowledge one and the same Son, our Lord Jesus Christ, at once complete in Godhead and complete in manhood, truly God and truly man...." This formula directly challenges every false claim of divinity by any human institution: state, church, cult, school, or human assembly. Christ alone is both God and man, the unique link between heaven and earth. All human power is therefore derivative: Christ alone can announce that "All power is given unto me in heaven and in earth" (Matthew 28:18). Historically, the Chalcedonian creed is therefore the foundation of Western liberty, for it sets limits on all authoritarian human institutions by acknowledging the validity of the claims of the One who is the source of true human freedom (Galatians 5:1).

The *Chalcedon Report* is published monthly and is sent to all who request it. All gifts to Chalcedon are tax deductible.

Chalcedon
Box 158
Vallecito, CA 95251 U.S.A.

Books by
R. J. Rushdoony

Romans & Galatians
Institutes of Biblical Law
Law & Society
Systematic Theology
The Politics of Guilt and Pity
Christianity and the State
Salvation and Godly Rule
The Messianic Character of American Education
Roots of Reconstruction
The One and the Many
Revolt Against Maturity
By What Standard?
Law & Liberty

For a complete listing of books by other
Christian Reconstructionists, contact:

ROSS HOUSE BOOKS
P. O. Box 67
Vallecito, CA 95251